24 WEEKEND
PROJECTS
FOR PETS

Doghouses, Cat Trees,
Rabbit Hutches
& More

by David Griffin

Creative Publishing
international

CHANHASSEN, MINNESOTA
www.creativepub.com

Creative Publishing international

Copyright © 2007
Creative Publishing international, Inc.
18705 Lake Drive East
Chanhassen, Minnesota 55317
1-800-328-3895
www.creativepub.com

Printed in China

10 9 8 7 6 5 4 3 2 1

Library of Congress Cataloging-in-Publication Data

Griffin, David
  Projects for pets : doghouses, cat trees, rabbit hutches & more / by David Griffin.
     p. cm.
  Summary: "Complete plans and instructions for building more than 20 habitats and furnishings for common household pets"--Provided by publisher.
  Includes index.
  ISBN-13: 978-1-58923-308-9 (soft cover)
  ISBN-10: 1-58923-308-5 (soft cover)
  1. Pets--Housing--Design and construction. 2. Pet supplies. I. Title.

  SF414.2.G75 2007
  690.89--dc22

2007003472

690.89

President/CEO: Ken Fund
VP for Sales & Marketing: Peter Ackroyd

Home Improvement Group

Publisher: Bryan Trandem
Managing Editor: Tracy Stanley
Senior Editor: Mark Johanson
Editor: Jennifer Gehlhar

Creative Director: Michele Lanci-Altomare
Senior Design Manager: Brad Springer
Design Managers: Jon Simpson, Mary Rohl

Director of Photography: Tim Himsel
Lead Photographer: Steve Galvin
Photo Coordinators: Julie Caruso, Joanne Wawra
Shop Manager: Randy Austin

Production Managers: Linda Halls, Laura Hokkanen

Page Layout Artist: Danielle Smith
Photographers: Andrea Rugg, Joel Schnell
Shop Help: Dan Anderson, Glenn Austin, Tami Helmer, John Webb

Special thanks to Leaping Lizards Reptile Shop of Burnsville, MN, for the loan of their snake, page 118. www.leapinglizardsreptileshop.com

24 Weekend Projects for Pets
Created by: The Editors of Creative Publishing international, Inc., in cooperation with Black & Decker.
Black & Decker® is a trademark of The Black & Decker Corporation and is used under license.

NOTICE TO READERS

For safety, use caution, care and good judgment when following the procedures described in this book. The Publisher and Black & Decker cannot assume responsibility for any damage to property or injury to persons as a result of misuse of the information provided.

The techniques shown in this book are general techniques for various applications. In some instances, additional techniques not shown in this book may be required. Always follow manufacturers' instructions included with products, since deviating from the directions may void warranties. The projects in this book vary widely as to skill levels required: some may not be appropriate for all do-it-yourselfers, and some may require professional help.

Consult your local Building Department for information on building permits, codes and other laws as they apply to your project.

Contents

24 Weekend Projects for Pet

Introduction

In recent years pet stores have changed from small mom-and-pop operations to big box superstores that peddle everything from guppies to automatic litter boxes to dog ramps to parrot perches. The advent of the pet store megamart has turned the special relationship between people and their companion animals into a multibillion-dollar industry. But unlike other retail markets that have undergone large-scale consolidation to a few big stores, the overall prices have not gone down as a result of economies of scale (if you've ever been charged $100 for a piece of thin foam wrapped in light fabric and called a dog bed, you'll agree).

Furthermore, anybody who's looked below the surface of pet store merchandise knows it's not Chippendale furniture. A typical cat condo, for example, is made of strand board, 2 × 4s and carpet remnants. Expensive reptile enclosures are fiberboard and Plexiglas. Dog kennels are little more than chain link panels tied together with pipe clamps.

This book is the culmination of research into pet structures that anybody with a few basic tools can make. We've intentionally kept the plans simple, but not so plain that they look completely homemade. Most projects require only basic hand tools, a circular saw and a drill/driver. The beauty of pet accoutrements is they don't have to be fancy. They just need to work well, be safe, look good, and make pets and their people happy.

Wherever possible, we've selected inexpensive commodity building materials—plywood, framing lumber, melamine-coated particleboard, hardware cloth—stuff that is common enough to keep the cost down. Yet we have specified oak, upholstery fabric and other "nice" materials for selected purposes where they'll make a difference. While we've tried to keep costs and difficulty low, we haven't settled for projects that are ugly or flimsy. To the contrary, we explain how to make sturdy, reliable products that in many cases outclass commercially available alternatives.

In short, we've done with these designs what you would have done if you had the time. We put careful thought and ample research into sizing, material safety, and functionality so you don't have to. That doesn't mean you can't innovate. Need an aviary that fits under the stairs? Modify our plan. Want to upholster a windowsill cat perch to match your couch? You can. One of the beauties of making it yourself is you can build it to suit your needs, your house and (most importantly) your pet's needs.

Perhaps the greatest pleasure of building pet structures is the creative outlet of the process. Cat climbers, thank goodness, aren't toasters; the only limits to their final appearance are the boundaries of your imagination (and a few assorted laws of physics). We hope you'll take the structural fundamentals of our plans and make the finished products your own and your pet's. Building a doghouse may have practical and economic advantages, but it's also an opportunity to let your inner artist shine.

Finally, let's not forget whom this book is all about: your pet! Making something he or she can use, for many, is act of love. It's a way of giving something back to our furry, scaly, or feathery friends. We've taken these animals into our care and they've enriched our lives. Let us, with our hands, make their time with us enriching too.

Tools & Materials for Pet Projects

Building homes and accessories for your pets can be accomplished with many of the same tools and building materials we use in our houses and landscapes. However, in some cases the fact that our pets are more inclined than our children to eat their house does impact the selection process. As with people-scale projects, you'll select materials for your pet projects based on safety, ease of use, appearance, durability, and cost. And most of the projects in this book can be constructed with simple hand and power tools that you probably own already. On the following pages we review some common materials with these considerations in mind. After that, you'll find a very brief refresher course on a few basic woodworking skills you'll need for even the most simple pet projects. Then, we jump feet-first into the pool of pet projects.

Every project in this book can be built with just a few ordinary hand and power tools you probably own already.

Building Materials for Your Pet Projects

SHEET GOODS

Sheet goods such as plywood and medium-density fiberboard (MDF) can be shaped easily with a router and some, especially MDF and medium-density overlay (MDO) feature a smooth surface that takes paint and contact paper well on both faces and edges. Machining most sheet goods produces hazardous dust that needs to be collected. To limit off-gassing of formaldehyde, use contact paper or apply sealing primer to sheet goods used for pet enclosures.

Interior plywood Frequently sold with a smooth, finish-grade hardwood veneer surface, plywood may be painted or sealed and stained. Plywood cuts easily and is the easiest sheet good to fasten. Hardwood plywoods are expensive and should be sealed to slow off-gassing of formaldehyde.

Exterior plywood and oriented-strand board (OSB) (sheathing, sub-floor decking) Panels are inexpensive and easy to fasten and cut. OSB and exterior plywood do not contain formaldehyde, making them preferable to hardwood plywood for unsealed carpeted cat structures and other interior structures where appearance is not an issue. Surfaces and edges are rough, and the plywood may not lie flat without framing.

Melamine Mostly available in white, melamine features a particleboard core and hard, water-resistant plastic faces that require no other paint or finish. Melamine is sometimes used as flooring for pet enclosures and cleanout trays. In this application, sides made from other materials are screwed and glued to the particleboard edges.

Common sheet goods that may be used for pets include hardboard (also available as perforated pegboard), MDF (medium-density fiberboard), and MDO (medium-density overlay).

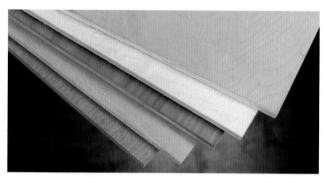

Interior plywoods often feature hardwood veneer and are generally higher quality than products made for exterior use. When used for pet projects (such as the aquarium stand on pages 124 to 129) make sure to seal them well with varnish or polyurethane, since they are created with adhesives and binders that will off-gas potentially dangerous fumes.

Sanded plywood, sheathing plywood and oriented-strand board (OSB) are economical project materials that can be painted, carpeted or used for other structural purposes.

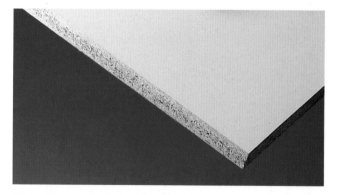

Melamine-coated particleboard has a tough, water-resistant (but also very slippery) surface coating that's applied at the factory.

WOOD

Softwood construction lumber. Stud grade
2 × 4s, 2 × 2 furring strips, lath, and construction
grade 1 × 3s are a few examples of construction
lumber that is safe, natural, easy to work with and
extremely inexpensive. With a little care, you can turn
these rough-and-tumble materials into pet projects
that belie their blue-collar pedigree.

    Cedar and redwood are naturally rot resistant
and hold paint well. Use for outdoor pet structures.
Find them in the fencing and decking sections of
home improvement stores. Do not use cedar shavings
as bedding for birds, reptiles, rabbits and pets that are
averse to strong smells.

    Hardwood is useful for any building project,
either for making the entire project or to trim out a
larger project made with sheet goods or softwood.

    Pressure-treated wood. Pressure-treated wood
no longer contains arsenic, as it once did. Use on
outdoor structures where proximity to soil may cause
rot. Avoid on parts of structures than may be chewed
by your pet.

    Manzanita wood. Natural manzanita branches
make durable, attractive, and safe perches for snakes,
lizards, and birds.

Species of lumber that are suitable for pet projects include
(clockwise from top): Redwood, pine, maple, oak, poplar,
dimensional framing lumber (spruce, pine or fir), and cedar.

Manzanita is a specialty wood sold at pet shops for its
premium perch-making qualities.

Pressure-treated lumber is usually a variety of pine and has
chemically enhanced resistance to rot and infestation.

METAL FABRICS

Galvanized hardware cloth. Galvanized hardware cloth is available in a range of mesh sizes and offers a strong, inexpensive cage material. The zinc in the coating can be toxic to birds, however. Scrub the surface zinc off in a 10% vinegar solution before using for birdcages. For cage-chewing birds, choose a different material.

Coated wire. Powder coated steel wire features a durable baked-on finish and is the next step up from galvanized mesh. Order it from wire mesh and animal enclosure suppliers with a suitable bar spacing to prevent entrapment of feet and heads. Note that determined chewers can break though a powder coat, sometimes exposing a dangerous zinc undercoat.

Stainless steel. Stainless steel is the gold standard of cage materials for birds and other pets, since there is no coating to be chewed off. It is also the most expensive. Special ordering is usually necessary.

Galvanized hardware cloth comes in a variety of grid sizes. Like any galvanized metal, it should be thoroughly washed with a 10% vinegar solution before using in an animal habitat.

MISCELLANEOUS MATERIALS

Plexiglas lends a professional, polished look to aviaries and reptile cages, while being easier to work with than glass. Use ¼" or thicker for snakes and large reptiles. Care must be taken to provide adequate ventilation, especially to birds.

Plastic tubing. Rodents such as gerbils and rats love tubes. A wide range of tubing is available from hardware stores and home centers. Larger-diameter PVC tubing can also be used as a structural element in cat condos and other accessories (see pages 106 to 110).

Paints, finishes, chemicals. Use water based, low volatile organic compound (V.O.C.) paints and finishes on pet projects then let cure until odor free. Birds are particularly sensitive to airborne chemicals emitted from paints, finishes, and cleaners.

Clear and unbreakable, Plexiglas is a very valuable material for observation cages such as this reptile cage (see pages 118 to 123).

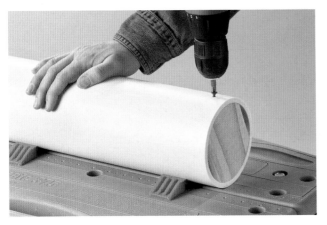

PVC tubing can be used as a tunnel for small animals or as a structural component.

Water-base or acrylic paints are safest for use around pets, but whichever finish materials you choose, read the product information very carefully.

Carpeting. Use dense, plush carpets without loops for cat projects. Fold and fasten the carpeting so cats and dogs can't chew the edges loose. Use carpet tacks or glue where cats might catch claws on staples. The CRI (Carpet and Rug Institute) Green Label is a plus if chemical odors are a concern.

Upholstery fabric. Any cat perch or dog bed can be given that sofa feel if you cover it with upholstery fabric and batting. Buy upholstery fabric and supplies at fabric stores. Rectangles and squares are easiest to upholster, since the fabric can be made smooth, folded under, and carpet-tacked or stapled to the bottom of the piece.

Sisal. Sisal rope and fabric are made from a tough, safe plant fiber. Use for cat scratchers, bird perches, and other pet project components likely to be shredded by your pet.

Carpet has many applications in pet projects. Look for a dense, non-looped weave.

Upholstery fabric is very sturdy and anyone who owns both furniture and a cat can attest to how much cats enjoy scratching it.

Sisal is a natural fiber rope, usually sold in 50-ft. rolls, that is perfect for cladding scratching posts and other cat accessories.

Woodworking Techniques

CUTTING

Circular saws and jig saws cut wood as the blade passes up through the material, which can cause splintering or chipping on the top face of the wood. For this reason, always cut with your workpiece facedown.

To ensure a straight cut with a circular saw, clamp a straightedge to your workpiece to guide the foot of the saw as you cut.

To make an internal cutout in your workpiece, drill starter holes near cutting lines, and use a jig saw to complete the cut.

A power miter saw is the best tool for making straight or angled cuts on narrow boards and trim pieces. This saw is especially helpful for cutting hardwood. An alternative is to use an inexpensive hand miter box fitted with a backsaw.

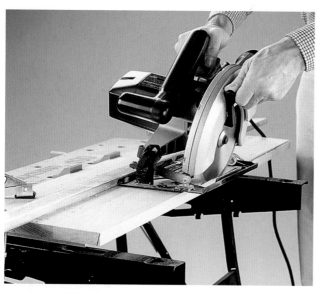

The foot of the circular saw rides along the straightedge to make straight, smooth cuts.

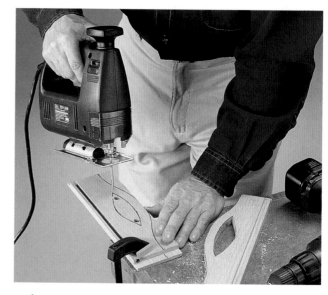

Make contoured cutouts by drilling starter holes and cutting with a jig saw.

A power miter saw is easy to use and quickly makes clean, accurate angle cuts in any wood.

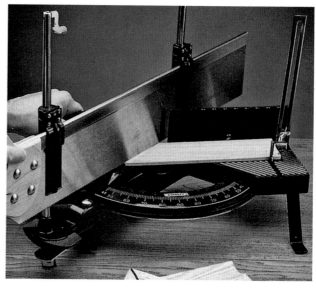

A hand miter box keeps your backsaw in line for making a full range of angle cuts.

Use a square grid pattern and a compass to draw patterns on your workpiece.

Clamp a belt sander and a scrap board to the workbench to create a stationary shaping tool.

SHAPING

Create detailed shapes by drawing a grid pattern on your workpiece. Use the grid to mark accurate centers and endpoints for the shapes you will cut. Make smooth roundovers and curves using a standard compass.

You can also create shapes by enlarging a drawing detail, using a photocopier and transferring the pattern to the workpiece.

A belt sander makes short work of sanding tasks and is also a powerful shaping tool. Mounting a belt sander to your workbench allows you to move and shape the workpiece freely—using both hands. Secure the sander by clamping the tool casing in a bench-top vise or with large handscrew or C-clamps. Clamp a scrap board to your bench to use as a platform, keeping the workpiece square and level with the sanding belt.

To ensure that matching pieces have an identical shape, clamp them together before shaping. This technique is known as gang-sanding.

Gang-sanding is an easy method for creating two or more identical parts.

SQUARING A FRAME

Squaring is an important technique in furniture construction. A frame or assembly that is not square will result in a piece that teeters on two legs or won't stand up straight. Always check an assembly for square before fastening the parts together.

To square a frame, measure diagonally from corner to corner. When the measurements are equal, the frame is square. Adjust the frame by applying inward pressure to diagonally opposite corners. A framing square or a combination square can also be used to see if two pieces form a right angle.

Clamp frame parts together. Then, measure the diagonals to check for square before fastening.

PILOTING AND DRILLING

Pilot holes make it easier to drive screws or nails into a workpiece since they remove some material, and keep the fastener from splitting the wood. If you find that your screws are still difficult to drive or that the wood splits, switch to a larger piloting bit. If the screws are not holding well or are stripping the pilot holes, use a smaller bit to pilot subsequent holes. When drilling pilot holes for finish nails, use a standard straight bit.

A combination pilot bit drills pilot holes for the threaded and unthreaded sections of the screw shank, as well as a counterbore recess that allows the screw to seat below the surface of the workpiece. The counterbore portion of the bit drills a 3/8"-dia. hole to accept a standard wood plug. A bit stop with a setscrew allows you to adjust the drilling depth.

When drilling a hole through a workpiece, clamp a scrap board to the piece on the side where the drill bit will exit. This "backer board" will prevent the bit from splintering the wood and is especially important when drilling large holes with a spade bit.

To make perfectly straight or uniform holes, mount your drill to a portable drill stand. The stand can be adjusted for drilling to a specific depth and angle.

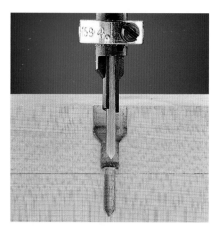

A combination pilot bit drills pilot holes and counterbores for wood screws in one step.

Use a scrap backer board to prevent tearout when drilling through a workpiece.

A portable drill stand helps you drill straight or angled holes.

GLUING

A gluing surface should be smooth and free of dust but not sanded. Glue and fasten boards soon after they are cut—machined surfaces, which dry out over time, bond best when they are freshly cut.

Before gluing, test-fit the pieces to ensure a proper fit. Then, clean the mating edges with a clean, dry cloth to remove dust.

Apply glue to both surfaces and spread it evenly, using a stick or your finger. Use enough glue to cover the area, with a small amount of excess.

Promptly assemble and clamp the pieces with enough clamps to apply even pressure to the joint. Watch the glue oozing from the joint to gauge the distribution of pressure. Excessive "squeeze-out" indicates that the clamps are too tight or that there is too much glue. Wipe away excess glue with a damp—not wet—cloth.

Clean the mating surfaces with a cloth to remove dust.

Spread glue evenly over the entire mating surface of each piece.

Set finish nails below the surface, using a nail set slightly smaller than the head of the nail.

Apply glue to wood plugs and insert them into screw counterbores to hide the screws.

Fill holes and wood defects with plain or tinted wood putty.

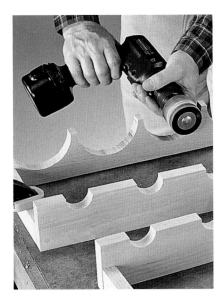

Smooth curves and hard-to-reach surfaces with a drum sander attachment on your power drill.

Draw pencil marks on veneered surfaces and sand only until they disappear to prevent oversanding.

PREPPING WOOD FOR FINISHING TOUCHES

Most projects require that nail heads be set below the surface of the wood, using a nail set. Choose a nail set with a point slightly smaller than the nail head.

Screws that have been driven well below the surface (about ¼") can be hidden by filling the counterbores with glued wood plugs. Tap the plug into place with a wood mallet or a hammer and scrap block, leaving the plug just above the surface. Then, sand the plug smooth with the surrounding surface.

Fill nail holes and small defects with wood putty. When applying a stain or clear finish to a project, use a tinted putty to match the wood and avoid smearing it outside the nail holes. Use putty to fill screw holes on painted projects.

A power drill with a sanding drum attachment helps you sand contoured surfaces until smooth.

Use a palm sander to finish-sand flat surfaces. To avoid sanding through thin veneers, draw light pencil marks on the surface and sand just until the marks disappear.

To finish-sand your projects, start with medium sandpaper (100- or 120-grit) and switch to increasingly finer papers (150- to 220-grit).

Cat Tree

A cat tree lets your cat scratch, climb and perch safely and harmlessly, which helps to preserve your furniture (and sanity) while keeping kitty healthy and happy.

Cover your new cat tree with upholstery batting and a tough upholstery fabric or dense non-looped carpet remnants, as we did here. We also stapled carpeting to cover the platforms. If fasteners need to be used on a gripping surface, use carpet tacks and glue. These won't snag your cat's claws as staples may. Apply catnip and hang toys from your tree to increase its attractiveness to kitty.

This cat tree is simple to build from framing lumber and a single sheet of ¾"-thick plywood. Rectangular components make this easy to carpet or upholster. The triple-ply base gives good heavy ballast to the structure (many cat trees you'll find suffer from tippiness). A ramp wrapped with sisal rope is perfect for climbing and scratching. This design includes offset platforms to allow jumping between levels. For carpet you may use practically any old scraps you have lying around the house. Generally, the denser the weave, the longer it will last. Avoid carpet with loops that can snag your cat's claws.

Tools

Stapler
Circular saw
Drill/driver
$1/8"$ drill bit
$3/16"$ drill bit
Driver bit
Hammer
Carpenter's square
Straightedge
Utility knife

Materials

5 to 6 yards of carpet remnants
   (allows for waste)
2 hinges with screws
One box $3\frac{1}{2}"$ deck or coarse-
   thread drywall screws
Wood glue
Carpet tacks
$9/16"$ staples
50 ft. roll of $3/8"$ sisal rope
Package of four $1\frac{1}{2}"$ threaded
   glides (feet)
(1) $3/4" \times 4 \times 8'$ construction
   grade (BC) plywood
(2) $2 \times 4 \times 8'$

Cutting List

Key	Part	Dimension	Pcs.	Material
A	Base	$3/4 \times 22 \times 26"$	3	Plywood
B	Base post	$3 \times 3\frac{1}{2} \times 16"$	1	Doubled 2×4
C	Tall base post	$3 \times 3\frac{1}{2} \times 28\frac{3}{4}"$	1	Doubled 2×4
D	Post	$3 \times 3\frac{1}{2} \times 12"$	4	Doubled 2×4
E	Level one	$3/4 \times 14 \times 14"$	1	Plywood

Key	Part	Dimension	Pcs.	Material
F	Level two	(L shaped)	1	Plywood
G	Level three	$3/4 \times 14 \times 26"$	1	Plywood
H	Level four	$3/4 \times 14 \times 16"$	1	Plywood
I	Ramp	$3/4 \times 5 \times 36"$	2	Plywood

How to Make a Cat Tree

Draw and label the panel components and cutting order onto the plywood sheet to avoid costly errors.

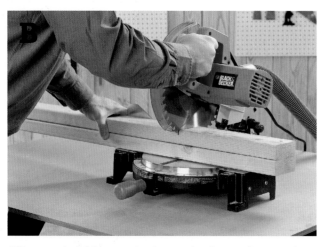

After sandwiching two 2 × 4s together face to face, cut the stock into post lengths.

Bevel the edge of the base at 22½ degrees.

MAKE THE PERCHES, POSTS AND BASE

Lay out the parts on your plywood sheet and cut with a circular saw (photo A). Cut the base and the platforms for the upper levels and the ramp. Glue, clamp and screw the two 2 × 4s together, face to face, to make a single 3 × 3½ × 8 ft. post. Use masonry blocks or five-gallon buckets filled with water to press the panels tightly together until the glue sets. Then, cut this post into the base post, tall base post, and intermediate posts (photo B). The tall base post is equal to 28" plus the thickness of your plywood. Remove any screws in the blade path before cutting. Glue the three base sections together.

ATTACH THE FIRST POSTS AND CARPETING

Face-glue the three-ply base and reinforce with wallboard screws. Then, cut a 22½° bevel on the base edge. The wide side of the base faces down (photo C). Position the short base post 9¼" in from a long side and 2" in from the front and position the tall base post 9¼" in from the same long side and 2" in from the back of the base. Outline them on the plywood base. Remove the posts and drill four ⅛" pilot holes, then tip the base over and drill counterbore holes at pilot hole locations, drilling through the bottom-most plywood panel.

Apply wood glue within the post outlines on the base and on the post bottoms. Have a helper hold the posts precisely in position. Attach from below with 3½" screws. Drive screw heads about one-third of the way into the base until they are firmly seated in the middle plywood layer (photo D). Cut a carpet piece large enough to overhang the base by 5" on each side. With a marker, transfer a map of the base top, including exact post locations, onto the back of the carpet. Make diagonal corner cuts 2" from the base corners. Cut along the lines, using a straightedge and a sharp utility knife on safe surface (photo E). Push the carpet down over the base so the posts penetrate the holes. Fold the carpet edges under the base and staple them from below. Hammer in any staples that aren't fully seated.

ATTACH LEVEL ONE

Trace the position of the posts onto the top and bottom of Level One and drill pilot holes. Attach the platform to the lower post through pilot holes, using glue and four 3½" screws. Then, drill angled pilot holes in the middle of all four sides of the upper post so you can attach it to the Level One platform toenail style (photo F). Cut and attach carpeting to the Level One platform.

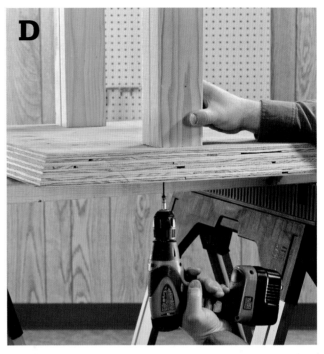

Countersink screws deeply into the base for better screw penetration of posts.

Cut scraps of carpet to fit the base. Outline and cut out holes for the posts.

Drill pilot holes near the base of the post and then attach the posts with glue and screws driven toenail style through the pilot holes.

Make relief cuts at corners so you can wrap the carpeting onto the platform.

Attach 4" butt hinges to the ends of the ramp. The hinges should be centered on the edge and on the same face of the ramp.

Preventing Unraveling ▸

Singe synthetic carpet edges over a flame before applying to "tie up" loose threads.

ATTACH LEVEL TWO

Trace the post positions onto the top and bottom of the Level Two platform and drill pilot holes. Place the Level Two platform top-face down on an upside-down carpet scrap and trace. Measure in from the edge lines to draw the post cutouts. Add an overlap and relief cut lines and then cut the carpeting (photo G). Attach posts and carpeting.

Tightly wound sisal rope coils that are slightly compressed create a durable scratching and climbing surface on the ramp. Use a 2 × 4 scrap to compress the rope as you bond it to the post.

Use carpet tacks on posts. Cardboard makes a safe holder for small fasteners, keeping your fingers clear of the hammer.

BUILD THE RAMP

Glue and weigh down two ramp-stock pieces, face to face. When the glue dries, cut the ramp to 34½" long. Pre-drill and screw hinges to the underside of the top and bottom of the ramp (photo H).

Nail one end of the ³⁄₈"-dia. sisal rope to the ramp, using carpet tacks driven along the width of the ramp. Wrap the ramp tightly with the rope (photo I). Compact the rope against itself with a block of wood as you go. After trimming, secure the last pull of rope to the ramp with carpet tacks. Holding the ramp vertically, screw the bottom set of hinge flaps to the base in a position that will allow the hinges at the top of the ramp to barely clear Level Two when they are folded down. Fold down the ramp to its final position and screw the top set of hinges to the bottom of the Level Two platform.

ATTACH THE REMAINING PLATFORMS

Attach and carpet the remaining levels. Cut panels of carpet 13" wide and as long as each post to carpet the posts. Center a carpet rectangle on the wide face of a post, glue, and nail it on with carpet tacks (photo J). Wrap carpet around the post and glue and tack it at the edges. Drill ¹¹⁄₃₂" (typically) holes in the corners of the base. Insert and adjust threaded glides (feet) so the structure doesn't wobble.

Green Doghouse

This "green" doghouse, with its sod roof and stucco siding, stays cooler in the summer and warmer in the winter. A sod roof, like the one featured, may become a favorite lookout perch for your pooch. Though this house is stucco, it could be sided to match your own house.

Tools

Measuring tape	Utility knife	Jig saw
Marker	Hammer	Clamps
Square	Caulk gun	Straightedge
Circular saw	Stapler	Trowel
Hand saw	Paintbrush	2" hole saw
Drill/driver		

Materials

(2) 8' pressure treated 2 × 4s
(1) 4' pressure treated 4 × 4
2 sheets 4 × 8' ¾" CDX plywood
1 half sheet (4 × 4') ¾" p.t. plywood
(3) 8' 2 × 3s (pine)
(6) 8' 2 × 2s (pine)
(1) 6' 1 × 3 (cedar)
(4) 10' 1 × 4 (cedar)
2" deck screws
3½" deck screws
2" galvanized casing nails
Staples
¾" roofing nails
36" long 2⁷⁄₁₆" drip edge
Two 2" circular louver vents
Roll 15 lb. building paper
½ sheet ⅝" cement board (optional)
Planting medium
Sod
12 ft. aluminum drip edge
3 × 12 ft. stucco lath
10 ft. stucco lath corner
Fencing staples

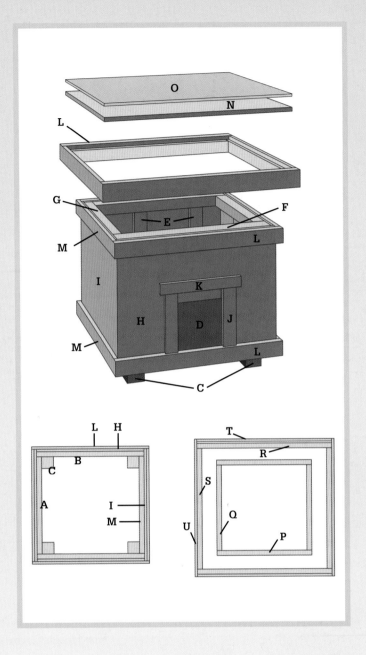

Cutting List

Key	Part	Dimensions	Pcs.	Material
A	Floor joist	1½ × 3½ × 29"	3	PT 2 × 4
B	Joist header	1½ × 3½ × 32"	2	PT 2 × 4
C	Feet	3½ × 3½ × 6"	4	PT 4 × 4
D	Floor deck	¾ × 32 × 32¾"	1	CDX plywood
E	Wall studs	1½ × 2½ × 22½"	9	2 × 3 Pine
F	Front & back top plate	1½ × 1½ × 32"	2	2 × 2 Pine
G	Side top plates	1½ × 1½ × 29"	2	2 × 2 Pine
H	Front/back wall sheathing	¾ × 32 × 27¾"	2	CDX plywood
I	Side wall sheathing	¾ × 33½ × 27¾"	2	CDX plywood
J	Door trim - side	¾ × 2½ × 12¼"	2	Cedar
K	Door trim - top	¾ × 2½ × 16¾"	1	Cedar

Key	Part	Dimensions	Pcs.	Material
L	Front/back frieze/base	¾ × 3½ × 35¼"	4	Cedar
M	Side frieze/base	¾ × 3½ × 33½"	4	Cedar
N	Roof deck	¾ × 39 × 40"	1	CDX plywood
O	Sod underlayment	⅝ × 39 × 40"	1	Cement board
P	Frame stops f/b	1½ × 1½ × 28½"	2	2 × 2 Pine
Q	Frame stops side	1½ × 1½ × 25½"	2	2 × 2 Pine
R	Deck frame f/b	1½ × 1½ × 39"	2	2 × 2 Pine
S	Deck frame side	1½ × 1½ × 36½"	2	2 × 2 Pine
T	Roof fascia f/b	¾ × 3½ × 40½"	2	Cedar
U	Roof fascia side	¾ × 3½ × 40½"	2	Cedar

How to Build a "Green" Doghouse

Drive deck screws through the second header and into the end of the outside joist, completing the 2 × 4 frame for the floor.

Finish the threshold tongue cutout, using a jig saw.

BUILD THE FLOOR AND STUD WALLS

Cut the floor joists and headers to length from pressure-treated 2 × 4 lumber. Drive a pair of 3½" deck screws through pilot holes in the ends of each header and into the outside joists to make a square frame (photo A). Use a carpenter's square to check for square. Press the corner into square if necessary, and then add the center joist between the headers.

Cut the floor deck to size from exterior grade (CDX) plywood. Start by cutting your plywood stock so it is 32 × 33½" in size. Then, draw a reference line ¾" back from and parallel to one long end. Measure in 11" from each end of the reference line and draw a cutting line that extends from the edge of the plywood to the reference line. Cut out the ¾" by 11" waste

section from each end, creating a ¾" × 10" tongue that will serve as the threshold of the doghouse (photo B).

Cut the wall studs to length. If your local lumberyard does not stock 2 × 3s, use full-width 2 × 4s, or rip-cut a 2 × 6 down the middle to create pairs of 2 × 3s (approximately). Position the studs on the top surface of the deck and trace around them for reference. Then, flip the deck on its edge and drive two or three 3½" deck screws up through the underside of the deck and into the bottom end of each stud (photo C). After all of the wall studs are attached to the deck floor, position the deck over the floor frame so all of the outside edges align. Drive 2" deck screws down through the plywood deck and into the tops of the floor frame members. Drive screws every 8" (photo D).

Cut the top plates for the front, back and side to length and then attach them to the tops of the wall studs with 3½" deck screws (photo E). Drill pilot holes first so you don't split the 2 × 2 plates. Test the stud walls with a framing square and adjust as necessary.

Flip the structure so the top plates are resting on a flat surface, then cut the feet to length. Attach the feet by driving a pair of 3½" screws through each 2 × 4 in the frame corner. The tops of the feet should be resting on the underside of the floor deck. It isn't necessary to drive screws down through the deck.

INSTALL THE SHEATHING AND TRIM

Cut the wall sheathing from ¾" CDX plywood. Use a circular saw and straightedge cutting guide or a table saw to make square cuts (photo F).

Outline the door opening in the front wall sheathing piece (see drawing, p. 23). Drill a starter hole in one corner of the cutout and then make the cutout with a jig saw, squaring off the corners as you go (photo G). If the cutout is uneven, smooth it with a belt sander or random orbit sander.

Drive a 3½" deck screw through the bottom of the floor deck and into a wall stud. Have a helper hold the stud, if possible.

Attach the deck (with the studs attached to the deck but loose on top) to the floor frame with deck screws.

Drive a deck screw down into the last top plate to complete the stud walls.

Cut out the wall sheathing panels from CDX plywood, using a circular saw and straightedge guide.

Drill starter holes and then make the door cutout in the front wall sheathing.

Attach the front piece of wall sheathing to the framing last.

Staple one long piece of building paper all around the doghouse, then trim the top. Cut out the door opening with a utility knife (cut from the inside, following the door opening edges).

Use galvanized finish nails to nail the front base trim piece in place.

Attach wall sheathing to the wall and floor framing with 1⅝" deck screws. Apply the front and back panels first. The threshold tongue should fit through the door opening (photo H).

Staple 15-pound building paper (use two layers for stucco) to the doghouse walls. Wrap the entire house with one course of building paper so the bottom edge of the paper is flush with the bottom edge of the sheathing. Staple the building paper every eight square inches or so, then trim off the excess at the top and cut out the door opening (photo I).

Cut the base trim boards to size. Using 2" galvanized finish nails, attach the front trim piece so

the top edge is flush with the top of the floor deck. The ends should overhang the sheathing by ¾" on each side (photo J).

Attach the side and back trim boards with finish nails, making sure the top edges of the trim boards are level with the top of the front base trim board.

Attach the top trim/frieze boards so the top edges are all even with the top edges of the sheathing and the stud wall caps. If the sheathing panels are not quite level with one another, install the trim so the tops are level with the lowest point on the wall sheathing and each board is parallel with the base trim beneath it.

Attach the head casing so the overhang on the side casing is equal.

Nail aluminum drip-edge flashing so it fits over the top edges of the base trim pieces.

Attach the two door casing trim pieces so they rest flush on the top edge of the base trim and are flush with the edges of the door opening. Cap the side trim pieces with the cap trim, centering the cap piece so the overhang is equal on both edges (it should be 1" per side) (photo K).

Mount a 2"-dia. hole saw in your power drill and drill two 2" holes into the back wall, centered side to side and about 2" down from the top. Insert 2" dia. circular louvers into the hole so the flange is about $\frac{3}{8}$" away from the wall on the outside of the doghouse. You'll need to work around the louvers as you install the stucco, but it is easier than trying to cut through the stucco after it is applied.

APPLY THE STUCCO FINISH

Using $\frac{1}{2}$" roofing nails, nail drip-edge flashing to the doghouse walls so the drip-edge covers and overhangs slightly the base trim. Make a relief cut and miter the corners of the flashing. The drip edge will direct moisture away from the trim pieces (photo L). Drill 2"-dia. vent holes near the top of the back panel and insert round, louvered vent covers (photo M).

Attach stucco lath (self-furring expanded metal lath) to the walls of the doghouse using galvanized fencing staples (photo N). At the corners, attach stucco edging using $1\frac{1}{2}$" roofing nails. Also attach edging (or drip screed) at the bottom edges of the walls. Cut the lath with aviator snips so it fits around the circular louvers on the back wall.

A traditional three-coat stucco finish is always best, but if you wish to take a shortcut here, trowel preformulated stucco mix over the lath, following the manufacturer's directions on the container (photo O). You can find this product at most home building centers or at your local concrete supplies dealer. Paint the stucco, if desired, after it has dried.

Tip ▸

To keep your grass roof groomed, don't use your lawnmower. Use a string trimmer, or give your rabbit a break from his hutch (page 38) and let him munch on the grass a few times each week.

M

Drill two 2"-dia. holes in the back panel, near the top to create openings for round louver vent covers.

N

Attach stucco edging to the corners of the doghouse, using 1½" roofing nails. Stucco lath should already be attached.

O

Apply premixed stucco (or a traditional stucco finish if you prefer) over the stucco lath according to the manufacturer's directions.

BUILD THE GRASS ROOF

The grass roof on this doghouse, while optional, is responsible for much of the structure's charm and efficiency. There is no standard way to construct a grass doghouse roof, but the main points are to make it leakproof, strong enough to support the sod, and to create some allowance for drainage.

Cut the plywood roof deck to size and coat it with waterproof deck sealer. Cut a piece of ⅝"-thick cement board to the same size. Cut cement board the same way you cut wallboard: score it with a utility knife and straightedge and then snap it over a 2 × 4 (photo P). The cement board is an optional underlayment for the sod. It is not waterproof, but it will not disintegrate and prevents the sod from skidding or sliding. You can use two or three layers of 6-mil plastic instead.

Cut the deck frame pieces to length and attach them around the underside of the deck frame by driving 1⅝" deck screws down through the plywood and into the frame pieces. Also cut and install the stop frame that will fit inside the roof opening, centering the frame so it will be inset 3½" from all edges of the plywood deck. To create controlled roof runoff, cut a piece of 2⁷⁄₁₆" drip-edge flashing the same length as the width of the roof deck (in the back). Nail the drip edge to the top, back edge of the plywood deck. Then, apply construction adhesive to the underside (the smooth side) of the cementboard and place it on top of the plywood, capturing the edge of the drip edge between the layers. Caulk around the edges.

Cut a subbase for the sod roof from cementboard or a waterproof membrane.

Drive galvanized finish nails through the back fascia and into the front ends of the side fascia pieces.

Cover the roof with sod. Unless you have a ready supply of replacement sod, lay down a layer (1" or so) of growing medium.

Cut the fascia to length. Attach the front fascia board with construction adhesive and 2" finish nails (galvanized) driven into the roof frame. The bottom edge of the fascia should be flush with the bottom edge of roof frame, leaving about ½" projecting above the surface of the roof deck. Attach the side fascia so the tops are flush with the front fascia, and then drive two nails through each end of the front fascia to lock-nail the side fascia pieces to it. Then attach the back fascia piece by driving finish nails through its face and into the ends of the side fascia boards. This should create a ½" drainage gap between the back fascia and the roof deck (photo Q).

Position the doghouse in your yard. To improve drainage, shim under the front legs about ¼" to pitch the doghouse toward the drainage gap in the back edge of the roof. Set the roof onto the house. Cut sod to fit and cover roof with it (photo R). Water sod frequently, as it will be vulnerable to drying out (positioning the house in partial shade will help prolong the life of the sod).

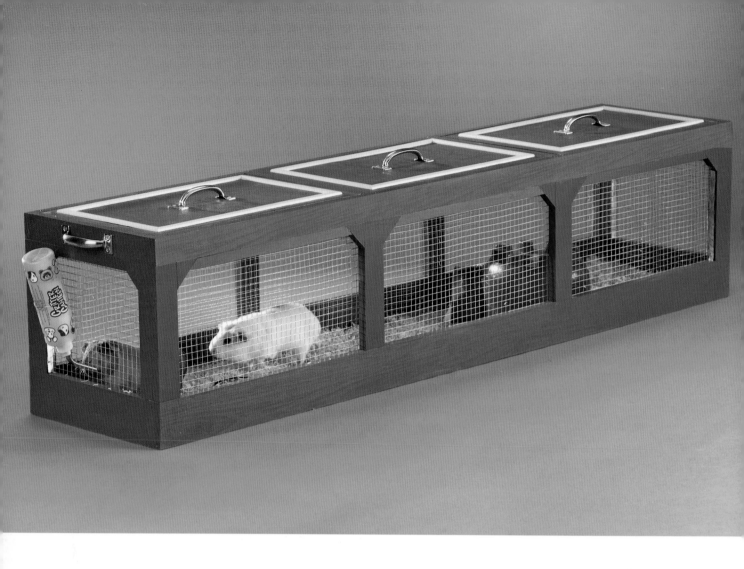

Small Animal Cage

Guinea pigs, ferrets, rats, and other small, furry pets require a bit more real estate than a small aquarium-size cage. Their available housing tends to fall into two categories: stark cages fabricated from metal hardware cloth, welded wire or mesh, or expensive plastic contraptions with coated wire walls. Both solutions leave a bit to be desired. If you long for a small animal cage that has the feel of home furnishings at the cost of a basic wire hutch, this cage project may be just the solution for you.

Because most small furry pets are gnawers, you don't want to leave any wood structural members exposed to the cage inhabitants. So the wood corner posts and stiles on this plan are clad with light-gauge aluminum flashing, preserving the appeal of a wood frame. The frame itself is made from paint-grade poplar, which is a durable wood that's naturally resistant to insects (hopefully, not something you need to be worrying about). We rip-cut some of the poplar parts to the exact dimensions we liked, but if you don't have access to a table saw, you can modify the design pretty easily so the entire project can be made from stock dimensional lumber.

The galvanized sheet metal tray that fits inside the cage was fabricated for us at a sheet metal shop for around $40. If you prefer, you can try to make your own 24"-wide roll flashing, which is sold in 10-ft. lengths at most building centers. It's considerably lighter than sheet metal, however, so you'll probably want to add a rigid panel, if not a complete wood box that you can line with the flashing. Overall size of the structure is 15" deep × 15½" high × 66" long.

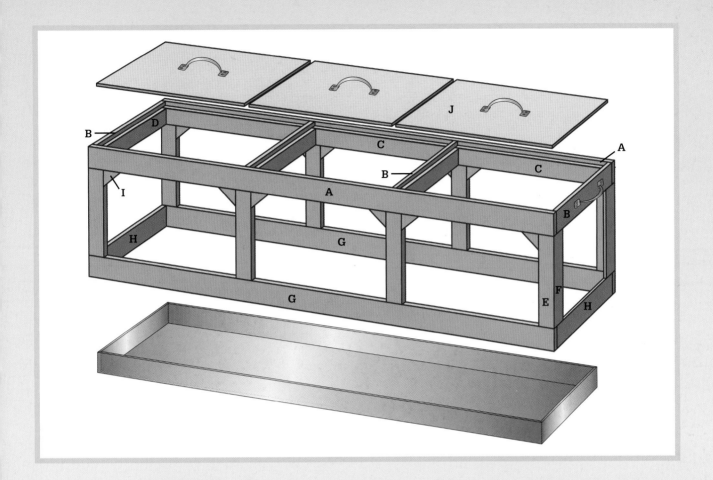

Materials

(5) 3" aluminum utility handles
Aluminum roll flashing
(2) 1 × 2" × 8' furring strips
(2) ½" × 8 ft. retainer molding

(3) 1 × 6 × 8 ft. poplar or pine
(1) ½" × 4 ft. × 4 ft. plywood
Aluminum brads
½" grid galvanized hardware cloth

Cutting List

Key	Part	Size	Pcs.	Material
A	Cover frame-front/back	³/₄ × 2 × 66"	2	Poplar
B	Cover rail	³/₄ × 2 × 13¹/₂"	4	Poplar
C	Cover ledge front/back	³/₄ × 1¹/₂ × 21"	6	1 × 2 Pine
D	Cover ledge - side	³/₄ × 1¹/₂ × 12"	6	1 × 2 Pine
E	Post	³/₄ × 2 × 10"	8	Poplar
F	Post filler	³/₄ × 1¹/₄ × 10"	4	Poplar
G	Bottom rail front/back	³/₄ × 3¹/₂ × 66"	2	Poplar
H	Bottom rail - side	³/₄ × 3¹/₂ × 13¹/₂"	2	Poplar
I	Corner block	³/₄ × 2 × 2"	16	Poplar
J	Lid	¹/₂ × 13¹/₄ × 20³/₄"	3	¹/₂" Plywood
K	Decorative lid trim	¹/₂"*		Half-round retainer molding
l	Metal tray	4 × 13 × 64"	1	Galvanized sheet metal

* Cut to fit

How to Build a Small Animal Cage

Rip nominal 1× poplar into 2"-wide strips (you'll need about 20 lineal feet 2" wide). Also rip stock to 3½" wide for the bottom rail pieces and the post filler strips. If you do not have access to a table saw, purchase three 8-ft. long 1 × 2 and two 8-ft.-long 1 × 4. Cut the parts to length. Create the corner posts by butting a post filler strip against a post at a right angle and attaching with glue and finish nails or pneumatic brad nails (photo A). Clamp the parts together to help make a cleaner joint. After the glue has set up, sand the joints to smooth out any irregularities.

Assemble the cover frame with glue and finish nails (photo B). Check the corners for square with a framing square. The two end rails should be installed between the front and back rails. The intermediate rails should be centered between the end rails. Once the cover frame is assembled and the glue has dried, cut the cap ledges from 1 × 2 pine furring strips. Attach the ledges inside the top frame openings so the bottoms are flush with the bottoms of the frame rails. This will create a ½"-deep recess for the ½"-thick lids to fit into.

Mark locations for the corner post assemblies and the intermediate posts on the top frame. Drill countersunk pilot holes through the top frame at each post location (two pilot holes per post). Set the posts in position beneath the frame and extend the pilot holes into the top ends of the posts. Attach the posts with glue and 3" wood screws (photo C). Once the top frame is attached to the posts, glue and nail the bottom frame parts together and, after the glue dries, attach the bottom frame to the bottoms of the posts with glue and 6d finish nails driven toenail style into pilot holes in the bottoms of the posts. Cut triangular nailing blocks (2" legs) from a 2"-thick strips and glue and nail them into the top and bottom corners of the wall frame bays (photo D). Be sure to drill pilot holes before nailing.

Fill nail and screw holes with wood putty; then sand the frame so the surfaces are smooth and the joints are even. Apply a coat of primer (photo E) and at least one coat of enamel paint (or finish with stain and polyurethane if you are using hardwood).

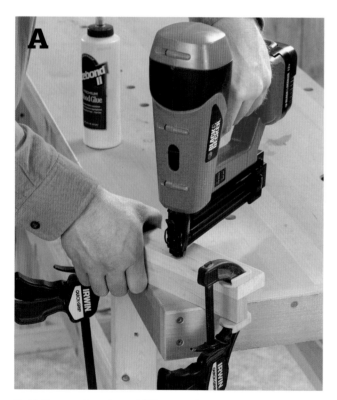

Butt the post and post filler together and join them with glue and nails.

Nail one of the intermediate rails between the end rails, which should already be attached. The frame should be standing on edge on the workbench.

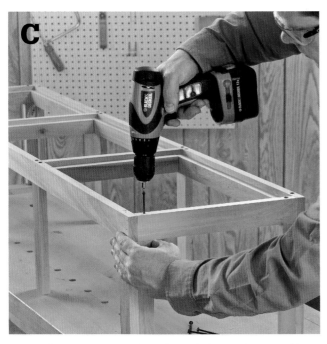

Drive 3" wood screws down through the top frame and into the tops of the corner posts.

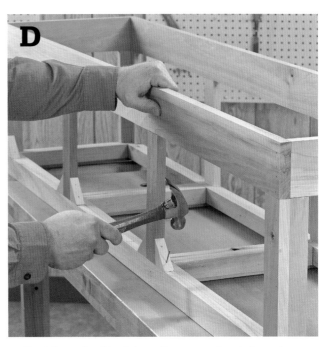

Nail a triangular block into all corners of each frame bay and assemble it upside down on your work surface.

Brush primer onto the wood to seal it before painting.

Material Usage Tip ▶

Rip 8 ft.-lengths of poplar 1 × 6 into 2"-wide strips on your table saw (or use a circular saw and straightedge). If you use nominal 1 × 6, with its actual size of 5¹/₂" wide, you can rip two 2" strips and a 1¹/₄" strip from each board.

To clad the inside post faces (not a critical step, but recommended), cut four strips of aluminum flashing to 3½" wide and 10" long for the corners. Crease the strips in half lengthwise and insert each piece of flashing into the inside angle of a frame corner. Nail the flashing to the wood surfaces with aluminum brads. Then, crease the free edges of the flashing so they fold crisply over the edges of the corner posts. Flatten the free ends against the post side and nail securely (photo F). For the intermediate posts, cut the flashing strips to 3 × 10" and crease the strips to conform to the back faces of the posts, nailing them on the side edges.

Cut the lids to size from ½"-thick plywood or particleboard. Paint the lids (a contrasting color can have a nice design impact here). For a decorative touch, make a mitered frame from half-round molding and glue and nail it to the top of each lid, inset about 1" from the lid edges (photo G).

Nail cladding (aluminum flashing) on the inside faces of the corner posts to discourage gnawing.

Make frames from mitered half-round molding (screen retainer is a good choice) and install them on the tops of the lids.

Install a 3" utility handle in the center of each lid. Also install handles at the top side frame members, centered front to back. Cut the fencing or hardware cloth into sections to fit the four walls. We used ½"-grid hardware cloth. Attach the fencing or cloth to each wall with fencing staples that are hammered into the backs of the posts and the frame (photo H). Make sure there are not sharp wire ends exposed.

Make (or have fabricated) a 4" high by 13"-wide by 64"-long sheet metal tray. We had ours made from 20-gauge galvanized sheet steel at a local sheet metal fabricator. Set the tray on the surface where you will be keeping the animal house (photo I). Line the tray with newspapers and bedding as you prefer, and then set the framed cage down onto the surface so it fits around the tray. You should not need to fasten the frame down. If your cage will house pets such as ferrets that climb and may try to escape the cage, add turnbuckle latches to hold the lids down.

Drive a ½" fencing staple through the hardware cloth or fencing and into a post.

Lower the cage down over the tray and set it in place.

Rabbit Hutch

This rabbit hutch is an easy-to-build outdoor shelter for your bunny. The floor is made of hardware cloth which allows droppings to fall through, but is easy on the rabbit's feet. A large airy compartment is enclosed with hardware cloth and a cozy smaller compartment is sided. Each compartment has a door to make feeding and cage cleaning an easier task.

Place straw or wood shavings in the compartment to make comfortable bedding for bunny.

Finish the rabbit hutch with an animal safe exterior stain. Place the hutch in a protected area out of direct sun.

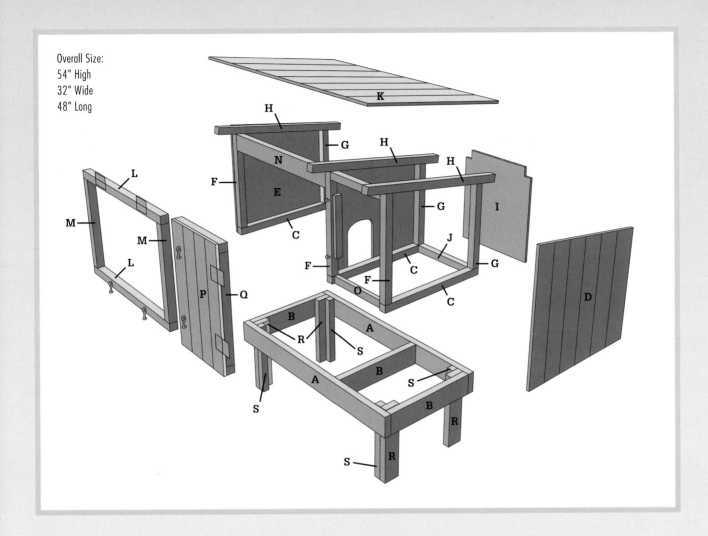

Overall Size:
54" High
32" Wide
48" Long

Materials

½" × 4 × 8' hardware cloth
¾" fence staples
1¼" and 2½" deck screws
(4) 3 × 3" hinges

(4) hook and eye fasteners
(7) 2 × 2" × 6' cedar
(7) 2 × 4" × 6' cedar
(1) ⅝" × 4 × 8' grooved cedar plywood siding (T1-11)

Cutting List

Key	Part	Dimension	Pcs.	Material
A	Floor side	$1\frac{1}{2} \times 3\frac{1}{2} \times 47\frac{1}{2}$"	2	Cedar
B	Floor crosspiece	$1\frac{1}{2} \times 3\frac{1}{2} \times 21$"	3	Cedar
C	Frame base	$1\frac{1}{2} \times 1\frac{1}{2} \times 24$"	3	Cedar
D	Right side wall	$\frac{1}{2} \times 24 \times 24$"	1	Siding
E	Left side wall	$\frac{1}{2} \times 24 \times 24$"	1	Siding
F	Frame front	$1\frac{1}{2} \times 1\frac{1}{2} \times 21$"*	3	Cedar
G	Frame back	$1\frac{1}{2} \times 1\frac{1}{2} \times 17\frac{1}{2}$"*	3	Cedar
H	Frame top	$1\frac{1}{2} \times 1\frac{1}{2} \times 32$"	3	Cedar
I	Back wall	$\frac{1}{2} \times 17\frac{1}{4} \times 20$"	1	Siding
J	Back wall stop	$1\frac{1}{2} \times 1\frac{1}{2} \times 13\frac{1}{4}$"	1	Siding

Key	Part	Dimension	Pcs.	Material
K	Roof	$\frac{1}{2} \times 32 \times 48$"	1	Siding
L	Door crosspiece	$1\frac{1}{2} \times 1\frac{1}{2} \times 29\frac{1}{2}$"*	2	Cedar
M	Door side	$1\frac{1}{2} \times 1\frac{1}{2} \times 17\frac{3}{4}$"*	2	Cedar
N	Hinge support	$1\frac{1}{2} \times 3\frac{1}{2} \times 29\frac{1}{2}$"*	1	Cedar
O	Door jamb	$1\frac{1}{2} \times 1\frac{1}{2} \times 13\frac{1}{4}$"*	1	Cedar
P	Compartment door	$\frac{1}{2} \times 13 \times 22\frac{1}{2}$"*	1	Siding
Q	Door supports	$1\frac{1}{2} \times 1\frac{1}{2} \times$ *	4	Cedar
R	Legs	$1\frac{1}{2} \times 3\frac{1}{2} \times$ *	4	Cedar
S	Legs	$1\frac{1}{2} \times 1\frac{1}{2} \times$ *	4	Cedar

*Cut to fit.

How to Build a Rabbit Hutch

BUILD THE FLOOR

For all screws in this project, drill a ⁹⁄₆₄" pilot hole and a ⅛"-deep counterbore.

Cut the floor sides and crosspieces. Mark a point 15¾" from the right ends of the side pieces.

Set the pieces on edge and apply exterior glue to the crosspiece ends. Drive 2½" deck screws through the sides into the ends. Center the third crosspiece at the mark and attach (photo A).

Cut a six-foot section of hardware cloth. Align one corner of the cloth with the right front corner of the floor. Attach it with ¾" fence staples every 4".

BUILD THE COMPARTMENT SIDES

Cut the frame bases and side walls. Place the walls together with the smooth sides facing in. Make a mark at 20" on a lengthwise side. Draw a line from the mark to the nearest opposite corner. Cut on the line to create the left and right peaked walls.

Make the door cutout on the inside wall by marking a 5 × 5" square 1½" up from the bottom and 4" from the front (longer) edge. Use a compass to draw an arch on top of the square. Drill a starter hole and use a jig saw to cut along the lines.

Align a frame base with the inside bottom of a wall. Attach the wall to the frame with 1¼" deck screws. Repeat with the second wall and base.

Draw a line across the inside of the walls, 1½" down from the peaked edge. Cut three sets of frame fronts and backs to fit between the frame base and the angled line. Attach using 1¼" deck screws through the siding into the frames.

Cut the frame tops. Center a top against each wall. Mark the ends so they are parallel with the sides and cut (photo B). Using one of these frame tops, cut the third frame top to match.

BUILD THE CAGE SIDE

Assemble the third set of frame pieces cut in the previous step. Drive 2½" deck screws through the frame base into the square ends of the frame front and frame back.

Center the frame top across the front and back. Make sure it matches the extension of the two compartment sides. Use 2½" deck screws to attach the top to the mitered ends of the front and back (photo C).

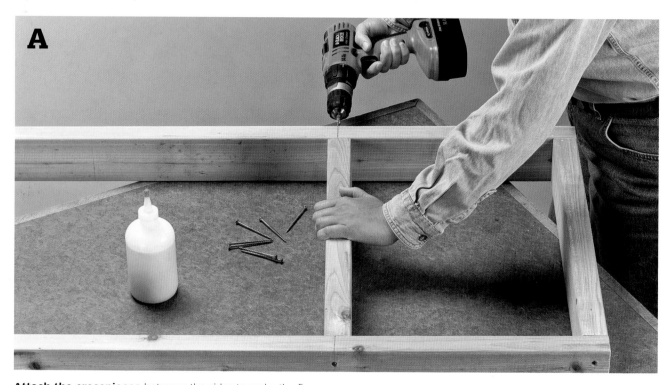

A

Attach the crosspieces between the sides to make the floor.

B

Center the frame top and mark the ends so they are parallel to the wall sides.

C

Attach the frame top to the frame back, sides, and base to create the cage side.

Attach the frames to the floor crosspieces.

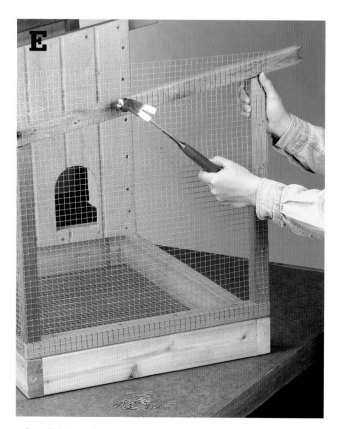

After folding and attaching the hardware cloth to the back, cut off excess cloth.

ATTACH THE FRAMES

Place the cage frame over the left floor crosspiece and attach using 2½" deck screws.

Place the sided frames on the middle and right end crosspiece, and attach using 2½" deck screws (photo D).

MAKE THE CAGE

Fold the hardware cloth against the back of the frames. Attach it to the left side frame and middle frame, using ¾" fencing staples every 4". Cut the hardware cloth along the edges of the middle and left end frame. Cut along the floor by the enclosed compartment and discard this piece.

Fold the hardware cloth up against the left frame and attach using ¾" fencing staples every 4" (photo E). Cut off the excess hardware cloth.

MAKE THE ROOF AND BACK WALL

Cut the back wall and back wall stop. Notch the wall upper corners to fit around the top frames.

Attach the stop to the floor between the side walls using 2½" deck screws. Attach the back to the back frames and stop with 1¼" deck screws.

Cut the roof, with the siding grooves oriented vertically. Attach the roof to the top frames with 1¼" deck screws (photo F).

MAKE THE DOORS

Measure the openings for the doors to make sure sizing is correct, then cut the door crosspieces, sides hinge support and door jamb.

Place the sides between the crosspieces, apply exterior glue and attach with 2½" deck screws. Cut hardware cloth to fit the frame and attach with ¾" fencing staples.

Position the door jamb between the compartment sides and attach with 2½" deck screws. Position the hinge support between the cage sides and attach with 2½" deck screws.

Cut the compartment door and door supports. Attach the door supports to the back of the door, using 1¼" deck screws.

Mount the doors with two 3" hinges each (photo G). Attach two hook and eye fasteners to secure each door.

ATTACH THE LEGS

Cut the legs to the desired length. Align a 2 × 2 against the wide side of a 2 × 4 to make an L. Use 2½" deck screws to attach. Attach the legs to the inside corners of the base with 2½" deck screws.

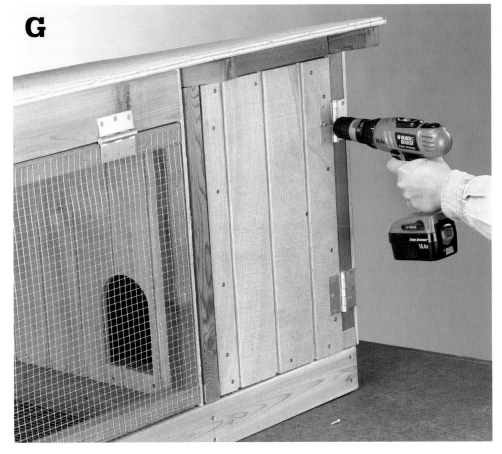

Attach the roof to the frames using 1¼" deck screws.

Mount the doors with 3" hinges.

Kennel Pergola

While chain link kennels are no substitute for outdoor exercise, they do provide a place for Fifi to relieve herself between trips to the dog park. Unfortunately, most basic kennel kits are just that—basic. Beautify your kennel with a pergola to provide shade or weather protection.

This kennel is made from prefabricated kennel panels readily available from home centers. Expand on the basic kennel below by adding more panels and a doghouse or sleeping platform. The lattice sun shelter may be embellished with climbing honeysuckle or wisteria vines, or replace the lattice with corrugated roofing for rain and snow protection. For your convenience, we'll show you how to build both roof types. This pergola design can easily be adapted to fit just about any size kennel you may already own.

Lattice panel

Tools

Measuring tape
Square
Circular saw
Drill/driver
Hammer

Materials

3" deck screws
1" galvanized box nails
2½" galvanized finish nails
(5) 2 × 4" × 8' cedar
(10) 2 × 2" × 8' cedar
(2) 1 × 3" × 8' cedar
(2) ⅜" × 4 × 8' lattice panels

Cutting List (for 6 ft. square kennel)

Key	Part	Dimension	Pcs.	Material
A	Rafter	$1\frac{1}{2} \times 3\frac{1}{2}" \times 8'$	5	Cedar
B	Purlin	$1\frac{1}{2} \times 1\frac{1}{2}" \times 8'$	5	Cedar
C	Spacer blocks	$1\frac{1}{2} \times 1\frac{1}{2}" \times *$	20	Cedar
D	Fascia	$\frac{3}{4} \times 2\frac{1}{2}" \times *$	2	Cedar

* Cut to fit. Measurements will need to be adjusted if 2 × 2s are less than 1½" square.

How to Build a Kennel Pergola

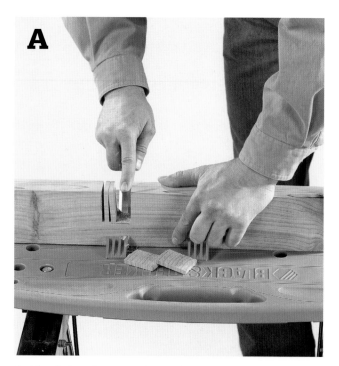

Cut kerfs into the area to be notched with a circular saw and then remove the remaining waste wood with a wood chisel.

SET THE RAFTERS

Measure the inside and outside width of the kennel at the top side rails, center these measurements on a rafter, then transfer to all the rafters with a square.

Notch the rail positions into the rafter with a series of cuts using a circular saw set to cut 2" deep. Clear out the wood between the saw kerfs with a hammer and chisel (photo A).

Fit the notched rafters over the side rails and space them evenly along the length of the kennel (photo B).

BUILD THE PERGOLA

The pergola is basically a grid of purlins that are supported by the rafters and in turn support either lattice or corrugated roof panels. Set the purlins onto the rafters, perpendicular to them and spaced evenly. Cut the spacer blocks to fit between the purlins at each end. The outer purlins should be about 3" from the ends of the rafters.

Pre-drill and screw the blocks and purlins to the rafters with deck screws (photo C).

Fit the notched rafters over the side panels of the kennel.

Drill pilot holes in the spacer blocks and purlins; then attach them to the tops of the rafters with 2½" deck screws.

Constructing a Kennel ▸

If you are also building the kennel, you'll need to follow the instructions that come with the kit you can purchase at your local building center. The pergola shown here is sized for a 6 ft. × 6 ft. kennel, which is the smallest size you can make with most kits. If you are building your kennel; locate your kennel on a well-drained concrete slab or patio pavers. If your dog will spend extended periods of time in the kennel, he must be provided with a dry sleeping platform protected from extreme heat and cold. See our doghouse entries. Attach the four walls of the kennel with two panel clamps at each corner. Note that the tension wire side of each panel faces down (see photo).

Kennel panels are assembled with the tension wire down to prevent your dog from pushing under the mesh.

D

Nail lattice panels to the purlins and blocking.

E

Nail the fascia boards to the ends of the purlins. The tops of the fascia boards should be flush with the top of the lattice panel.

Lay the lattice panels over the framework flush or within the ends of the purlins. Pre-drill and nail the lattice to the structure with galvanized box nails (photo D).

Attach the fascia boards to the ends of the purlins and rafters with 2½" galvanized finish nails. The fascia should overlap the lattice panel ends and hang below the purlins (photo E).

Seal the cedar lumber with waterproof deck sealer, preferably containing a UV inhibitor.

Corrugated Roof Option ▸

For rain and snow protection, attach four sheets of 2 × 8 ft. corrugated fiberglass roofing to the top of the pergola framework instead of lattice. Make the following adjustments:

- Use 2 × 6 instead of 2 × 4 rafters and wire the rafters to the kennel.
- Skip the blocking between purlins, but add an additional purlin. Align end purlins 1½" from rafter ends; then space the other purlins evenly in between.
- Screw wooden moldings with a corrugated profile to the tops of the purlins.
- Position roofing so the corrugations end on a downswing and overlap each other by one or two corrugations.
- Trim purlins so the moldings end on an upswing, one-half corrugation inside roofing edges.
- Push front and back fascia up into overhanging corrugation for support.

Drive screws or nails with rubber washers into a hole drilled at an angle into the roof/fascia/purlin. Note that the edge screws are driven at an angle into the fascia; otherwise, drill and screw at the peak of the corrugations. Pre-drill and fasten roofing to moldings at every other crown (top) of corrugations.

Cat Climber

Cat walks, steps, climbers—whatever you call them—cats love them. It's in their genes to get up high. These are offset from the wall for two-sided gripping and better wall clearance for turning. Unfinished or stained wood provides good traction, or you can carpet the ledges for grip with comfort. Remember that any path prefers a destination. Our plan calls for a regal corner perch high above the room.

Toggle bolts are used to connect the step brackets to the wall, which provide plenty of strength. Unless you have very heavy cats, or your children will do some climbing, stud attachment is not required.

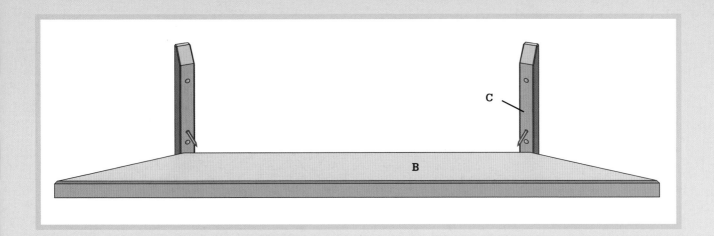

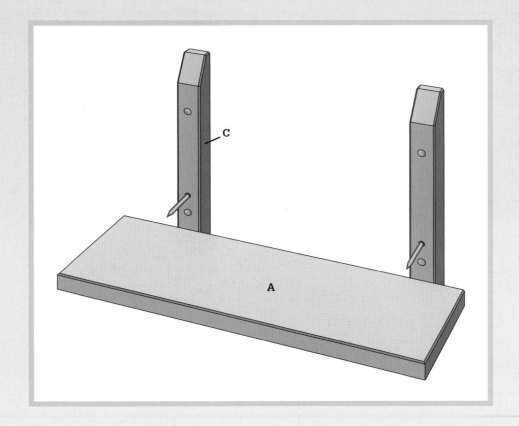

Tools

Measuring tape
Miter square
Table saw*
Belt sander* or rasp
Vise, drill
Countersink bit
Drill bits
*optional

Materials

Painter's tape
Cardboard scraps
$3/8 \times 3 1/2$" lag bolts
$1/8 \times 3$" toggle bolts
Wood dowel
Wood glue
(2) 2×6" (24" per ledge,
    48" per perch)
(1) 2×4" (24" per ledge
    or perch)

Cutting List

Key	Part	Dimension	Pcs.	Material
A	Ledge	$1 1/2 \times 5 1/2 \times 24$"	6	Pine
B	Perch	$1 1/2 \times 5 1/2 \times 48$"	1	Pine
C	Bracket	$1 1/2 \times 1 1/2 \times 12$"	*2 per step	Pine

How to Build a Cat Climber

Careful mapping is key to a cat climber that will work for your cats and not create an obstacle course for your humans.

Bevels can be tricky. Scribe a line with a combination square 3/16" in from the edges. This mitered bracket end is easiest beveled with a rasp or a belt sander.

MAP LEDGE AND PERCH LOCATIONS

Start with the corner perch. Use two pieces of 36" painter's tape to represent the wall space occupied by the corner perch near the ceiling.

Use six 24" pieces of tape to map a route of ledges to and from the corner perch. Consider your cat's leaping ability when spacing the ledges, both vertically and horizontally.

Tool Tip ▸

You may make your beveled and square rip cuts with a circular saw. Use a clamped straightedged board to run your saw against. For the bevels, provide an extra board under the body of your saw as a runner, since the saw will ride to the outside of the cut.

Adjust the lengths of the ledges if needed by cutting or adding to your tape and altering the ledge cut list. Mock up the shelves with cardboard and tape to see if they'll get in your way. The real shelves will project 7" into the room (photo A).

CUT LEDGES AND BRACKETS

With a table saw set to 45 degrees, rip cut 3/16" off each long edge corner of the 2 × 6 and 2 × 4 stock.

Cut the ledges and perch to length. Cut 45° ends on the perch so it will fit in a corner. (If your house is older, check the corner to see if it is square. If not, adjust the perch miters to fit the walls.) Rip the beveled 2 × 4 into two sticks of equal width, then cut the brackets to size. Measure 3/8" out from the flat sides of the brackets. Cut 45° ends at the marks. Cut, sand or rasp bevels on the end cuts of ledges and brackets (photo B). Note that brackets have bevels on the room side, not on the wall side.

ASSEMBLE THE LEDGES

Mark the ledges 3" in from each end. Clamp a ledge in a padded vise. Measure 4" down from one end of each bracket and mark with a try square. Align this bracket mark against the ledge at the mark.

Drill a 3½"-deep pilot hole with a ¼" bit through the back of the bracket and into the ledge. Counterbore a ½" hole to the depth of the lag bolt head and drill a ⅜" clearance hole through the bracket. Fasten the bracket to the shelf with a ⅜ × 3½" lag bolt (photo C). Repeat to attach the brackets to the shelves. On the corner perch, the brackets are attached midway on the mitered ends of the perch so that each bracket faces a different wall. Sand and finish the cat climber as desired.

INSTALL THE CAT CLIMBER

It is easiest to do this step with an assistant.

Mark mounting bolt positions 3" in from the bottom and 2" in from the top of each bracket. Hold a ledge in position on your wall layout tape. Make sure the ledge is level and drill 3/16" holes through the brackets into the wall. Drill counterbores for the bolt heads (photo D).

Remove the shelf and extend 3/16" holes through the plaster and lath or sheetrock. If you encounter a wood stud, stop drilling. If you encounter hollow wall, change bits and expand the holes to 9/16".

If you've encountered a stud, secure the bracket to the stud with 3½" drywall or deck screws. Otherwise, put toggle bolts and toggles on both brackets.

Push the toggles into wall so they open within the wall and tighten. Level the shelf again before final tightening, since toggle bolts allow play. Glue dowels in the screw holes and cut the tops flush to the bracket surface with a fine-tooth saw. Apply wood finish.

Tool Tip ▸

A bolt driver bit in your drill/driver makes driving lag bolts a snap.

Tool Tip ▸

For removable screw covers, buy wood-screw buttons from a woodworkers supply store and secure with a small dab of glue.

Draw your positioning lines on each ledge and brackets so they are visible as you drill for your bolts.

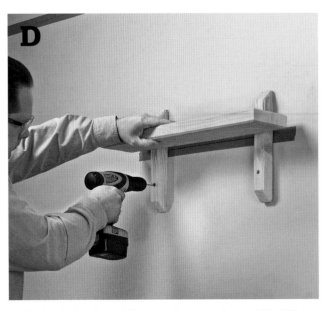

Hold the ledge in position over the layout tape while drilling pilot holes.

Utility Doghouse

Flat roof utility doghouses are found throughout the world. Often constructed with a slight slope to the roof, they are easy to insulate and, when sized appropriately, keep dogs warmer than a house with a peaked roof. In the summer, the roof may be propped open slightly for ventilation. The inner partition may also be omitted in southern climes. In the wintry north, a canvas door flap will help keep in the heat. Regardless of where you live, keep the sleeping area bedded with fresh straw or cedar shavings.

The doghouse shown here has a simple exterior plywood roof that I sealed with three coats of enamel porch paint. If the climate in your area is wet or cold, adding a roof covering, such as fully bonded asphalt roll roofing, is advisable. The interior walls and ceiling of the sleeping area are insulated and have hardboard wallcoverings as shown. This is an optional detail.

Tools

Measuring tape
Marker
Square
Circular saw
Drill/driver
Utility knife (with 2" or larger blade)
Hammer
Caulk gun
Paintbrush
Brad nailer (optional)

Materials

Deck screws
Box nails
Caulk
Panel adhesive
Exterior primer and paint
Hinges (3)
1½" galvanized casing nails
(2) 2 × 4" × 10' pressure treated pine
(6) 2 × 2" × 8' framing lumber
½" sheet of ¾" exterior plywood
(2) ½" × 4 × 8' exterior plywood
(1) 1½" × 4 × 8' rigid foam insulation
    (optional)
(1) ⅛" × 4 × 8' tempered hardboard
    (optional)

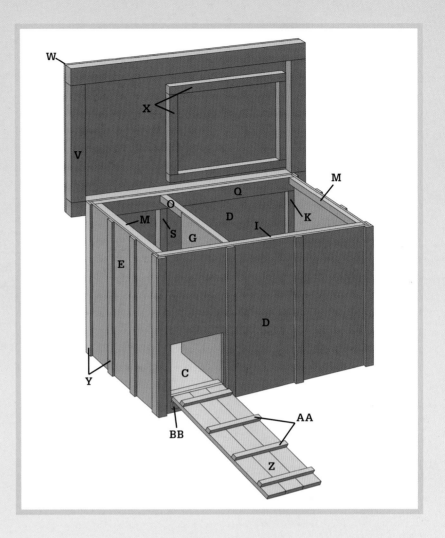

Cutting List

Key	Part	Dimension	Pcs.	Material
A	Joists	1½ × 3½ × 29"	4	Pressure treated
B	Rim joists	1½ × 3½ × 48"	2	Pressure treated
C	Floor	¾ × 48 × 32"	1	¾" Plywood
D	Front and back wall	¾ × 30/33 × 48"	2	½" Plywood
E	Tall wall	½ × 33 × 33"	1	½" Plywood
F	Short wall	½ × 30 × 33"	1	½" Plywood
G	Partition wall	½ × 30 × 19"	1	½" Plywood
H	Left stud front wall	1½ × 1½ × 27⅞"	1	Pine
I	Top plate front wall	1½ × 1½ × 48"	1	Pine
J	Right stud front wall	1½ × 1½ × 25"	1	Pine
K	Middle stud front wall	1½ × 1½ × 27"	1	Pine
L	Sill plate front wall	1½ × 1½ × 48"	1	Pine
M	Sill and top plate, tall & short walls	1½ × 1½ × 29"	4	Pine
N	Studs for partition	1½ × 1½ × 27"	2	Pine

Key	Part	Dimension	Pcs.	Material
O	Top plate partition	1½ × 1½ × 29"	1	Pine
P	Bottom plate partition	1½ × 1½ × 19"	1	Pine
Q	Back wall top plate, hinge side	1½ × 3½ × 48"	1	Pine
R	Back wall right stud	1½ × 1½ × 23"	1	Pine
S	Back wall middle stud	1½ × 1½ × 25"	1	Pine
T	Back wall left stud	1½ × 1½ × 26"	1	Pine
U	Roof	½ × 56 × 41"	1	½" Plywood
V	Flat-to-roof edge frame	1½ × 3½ × 34"	2	Pine
W	Flat-to-roof edge frame	1½ × 3½ × 56"	2	Pine
X	Roof insulation frame	1½ × 1½ × *	4	Pine
Y	Siding batten	¾ × 1½ × *	16	Pine
Z	Ramp board	1½ × 3½ × 36"	3	Pine
AA	Ramp tread	¾ × 1½ × 9"	4	Pine
BB	Ramp cleat	¾ × 1½ × 10"	1	Pine

* Cut to fit.

How to Build a Utility Doghouse

Connect the rim joists and the floor joists with 3" deck screws. For pressure-treated lumber, be sure to use stainless steel, hot-dipped galvanized, or coated screws.

Lay out the trapezoidal shapes for the side walls and cut the panels to size and shape with a circular saw and straightedge cutting guide.

BUILD THE FLOOR AND WALLS

The floor is made of exterior grade ¾" plywood set onto 2 × 4 pressure-treated joists. The joists are offset slightly so the partition wall can be located above a joist when it is installed. Cut the joists and rim joists to size length. Lay out the joists between the rim joists with one at each end and the others located 14" in from the ends. Drill pilot holes and drive two 3" screws through the rim joists into each joist end (photo A).

Cut the floor and wall panels to size using a circular saw and straightedge (photo B). Note that the front and back walls slope downwards from 33" high to 30" high to create a slight roof pitch for rain and snow runoff. Cut the panels so that when the house is assembled, the better grade face on the plywood will be facing out.

On the back face of the front wall panel, outline the door 3" from the left edge of the wall (when

Minimum/Maximum Sizing ▶

This house fits a medium-size dog like a Springer Spaniel or Border Collie. Adjust the dimensions of your doghouse to the size of your dog. At minimum:

- The bottom-to-top height of the door opening must equal the depth (D) of your dog plus 1".
- The length and width of the sleeping area must approximately equal the length (L) of the dog from nose to rump (tail excluded).
- The height of the ceiling should exceed the dog's standing height (H) by 25%.

If the dog will use the house to stay warm, do not exceed minimum sizing by more than 25%.

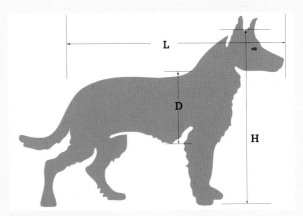

Dogs need less room than you might expect, and benefit in cold weather from a close-fitting house.

Cut out the door opening with a jig saw. You can either make a plunge cut with the saw or drill a starter hole for the saw blade.

viewed from the outside of the doghouse) and 3½" up from the bottom. Size the opening according to your dog's height (see "Minimum/Maximum Sizing," above). Drill a starter hole in the outline. Use a jig saw to cut the door opening (photo C), squaring off the corners once the waste has been cut out.

Cut the framing members to size except for the front and back top plates. Draw lines on the inside

faces of the wall panels, 2" up from the bottoms (photo D). Attach the sills above these lines with 1⅝" screws from the outside. Use this method to attach all framing to the walls. On the side-wall sills, leave a 2" gap between the sill ends and the sides of the panels. Attach the side-wall top plates to the top insides of the walls, also leaving a 2" gap at the plate ends.

Attach the studs to the front and back wall panels (photo E). Align the left and right studs with the ends of the panel. Align the middle studs between lines 33" and 34½" from the high side of the panels. Note that the back studs are shorter than the front studs to accommodate the 2 × 4 top plate. Cut the front and back top plates to fit and attach. You may trace the angle lines directly on the plates by positioning them in the walls.

ATTACH THE WALLS

Attach the wall sections to the deck with 2½" screws driven every 8" through the sill plates. Attach the side walls to the front and back walls by driving 2" screws through the plywood into the framing. Attach the partition wall to the partition wall framing. Align the partition wall ¾" offset from the middle stud, so the hardboard interior can be attached to the studs later (photo F). Attach the partition wall to the floor (photo G).

Lay out locations for the individual wall framing members on the inside surfaces of the wall panels.

Attach each individual wall panel to the wall framing members with deck screws driven through the sheathing and into the wall panels.

Pre-drill pilot holes into the offset partition and wall studs and attach the wall with 3" screws. The offset provides attachment surfaces on both walls for hardboard insulation covering.

Secure the sill plate for the partition wall to the doghouse floor with deck screws.

Attach three utility hinges, spaced evenly, along the back wall and roof perimeter frame. The barrels of the hinges should be 1½" beneath the top edge of the back wall.

Cut pieces of 1½"-thick rigid foam insulation board to fit into the stud wall cavities and roof frame. Score the insulation with a utility knife and snap or cut it with a wallboard saw.

BUILD & INSTALL THE ROOF

Cut the plywood roof panel to size and the 2 × 4 roof frame members to length. The roof framing is aligned with the perimeter of the roof and is attached with the 2 × 4 faces against the underside of the roof. Attach the framing to the roof. Cut the roof insulation frames to size so the square frame fits inside the sleeping area walls when the roof is closed. Test-fit the roof. There should be approximately a ½" gap between the roof framing and the wall sides. Install the roof framing. Screw three utility hinges to the back exterior wall panel, located 1½" down from the top of the wall sheathing (photo H).

INSULATE & COVER WALLS

Cut 1½"-thick rigid foam insulation board into panels that fit within the stud wall openings inside the sleeping area (photo I). Use a utility knife or a wallboard saw to cut the insulation. Also cut insulation board to fit inside the ceiling frame on the underside of the roof panel. Using a non-solvent based panel adhesive, attach the insulation to the walls, roof and underside of the floor. Then, cut wall and ceiling coverings from ⅛"- or ¼"-thick tempered wall panels. Install the wall panels with 1" brads (photo J).

FINISH THE HOUSE

As a decorative touch, cut 1 × 2 battens to fit on the walls and at the corners, extending from the bottom to the top of the wall sheathing. Nail a batten at each corner and add two intermediate battens, evenly spaced, per wall (photo K). If your dog is on the small side, build him or her a ramp from 2 × 4 and 1 × 2 scrap, then screw the top end of the ramp to a 1 × 2 cleat mounted beneath the door opening (photo L). If you have a larger dog, don't install a ramp—it will only be an impediment.

Prime, paint or stain the house. For the roof, apply at least three coats of exterior enamel porch paint. Ideally, you should position the doghouse in a sheltered spot in your yard.

Cover the walls inside the sleeping area with tempered hardboard panels. Also cover the ceiling insulation and frame with hardboard.

Cut strips of 1 × 2 pine to create battens that fit between the bottoms and tops of the exterior sheathing. Install four battens per side, spaced evenly and at each corner.

Paint the doghouse and the battens with exterior paint. If you own a smaller dog, build a simple ramp from 2 × 4 and 1 × 2 scraps, paint it to match, and attach it to a cleat beneath the door opening.

Indoor Aviary

Indoor aviaries are ideal for small communities of finches and other songbirds. Horizontal space is considered premium for such birds, which happily fly from perch to perch across the cage. Though vertical space is less valued, your birds will be calmer if they can perch higher than most people and other pets stand. Finches and other songbirds need full-spectrum light to stay healthy and strong. Full-spectrum fluorescent lights may be put on timers and mounted to the top of your aviary to mimic natural day length.

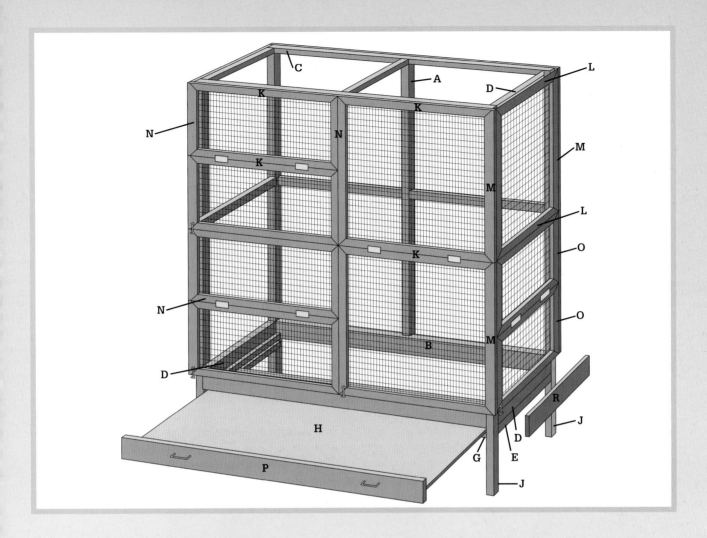

Tools

Measuring tape
Tin snips
Framing square
Drill driver
Miter square
Hammer
Circular saw
1/2" countersink bit
Miter box and saw
Assorted driver
    and drill bits
Corner clamps
Staple gun
Utility knife
Screwdrivers

Materials

(7) 2 × 2" × 8 ft. cedar
(2) 2 × 4" × 8 ft. cedar
(13) 1 × 2" × 8 ft. poplar
(4) 1 × 4" × 8 ft. poplar
(1) 1/2" × 4 × 8 ft. plywood
(1) 2 ft. × 50 ft. roll of 1/4"
    hardware cloth
1/2" hardwood dowel
Glue
Finish nails
Deck screws
9/16" staples
(8) brass butt hinges (2 × 2 1/2")
(4) eye hooks hooks and eyes
(2) door or drawer pulls
1 roll contact paper

Cutting List

Key	Part	Dimension	Pcs.	Material
A	Frame upright	1 1/2 × 1 1/2 × 45"	2	2 × 2 Cedar
B	Frame front/back base	1 1/2 × 3 1/2 × 45"	2	2 × 4 Cedar
C	Frame front/back top	1 1/2 × 1 1/2 × 48"	2	2 × 2 Cedar
D	Frame side bottom	1 1/2 × 3 1/2 × 21"	2	2 × 4 Cedar
E	Drawer support	1 1/2 × 1 1/2 × 21"	5	2 × 2 Cedar
G	Drawer guides	1/2 × 1/2 × 24"	4	Poplar
H	Drawer bottom	24 × 44 3/4 × 1/2"	1	1/2" Plywood
J	Leg/frame upright	1 1/2 × 1 1/2 × 66"	4	2 × 2 Cedar
K	Face frame piece	3/4 × 1 1/2 × 23 7/8"	20	1 × 2 Poplar
L	Face frame piece	3/4 × 1 1/2 × 24"	22	1 × 2 Poplar
M	Face frame piece	3/4 × 2 1/2 × 24"	6	1 × 3 Poplar
N	Face frame piece	3/4 × 1 1/2 × 12"	8	1 × 2 Poplar
O	Face frame piece	3/4 × 2 1/2 × 12"	4	1 × 3 Poplar
P	Front and back base trim	3/4 × 3 1/2 × 46 1/2"	2	1 × 4 Poplar
R	Side base trim	3/4 × 3 1/2 × 25 1/2"	2	1 × 4 Poplar

How to Build an Indoor Aviary

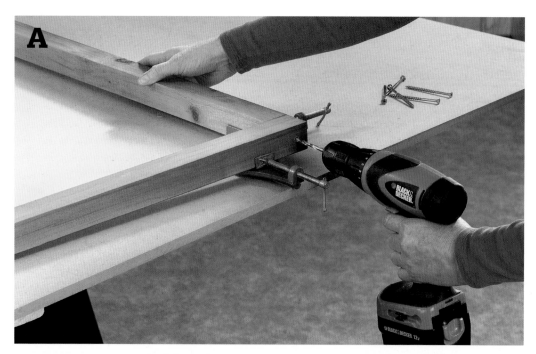

Attach the frame members with deck screws driven into pilot holes. A corner clamp is useful for holding pieces in place for gluing and fastening.

Connect each central upright to the base frame below with 1¼" screws driven through a metal T-bracket connector. Use a carpenter's square or framing square to check for square.

BUILD THE STRUCTURAL FRAME

The aviary has an internal framework of 2 × 2 and 2 × 4 cedar from which the wire-clad face-frame panels are suspended. Some of the panels are hinged and other are fixed. A plywood tray slides out of the bottom for easy cleaning.

Cut the structural frame pieces to length. On a large, flat surface, lay out two legs, a base, an upright, and a top frame member to make the front frame. A corner clamp is helpful for alignment while drilling pilot holes (photo A). Attach the upright to the midpoint of the base using glue and a T-bracket (photo B). Attach the legs to the base with glue and two 3" deck screws. Drill pilot holes and countersink all screw heads. Attach the top to the top of the legs

Building Materials Toxicity ▶

Compounds found in common building materials can irritate and kill caged birds.

- Zinc is toxic to birds. Consider purchasing stainless steel or coated mesh from a wire mesh supplier. If you use galvanized wire mesh, scrub off residual zinc in white vinegar; then wash with soap and water.

- Cedar wood can irritate caged birds. Seal cedar cage frames.
- Use low Volatile Organic Compound (VOC) non-toxic sealants and paints; let structure cure until odor-free before using.
- Line clean-out drawer with paper only. Do not use cat litter or wood shavings.

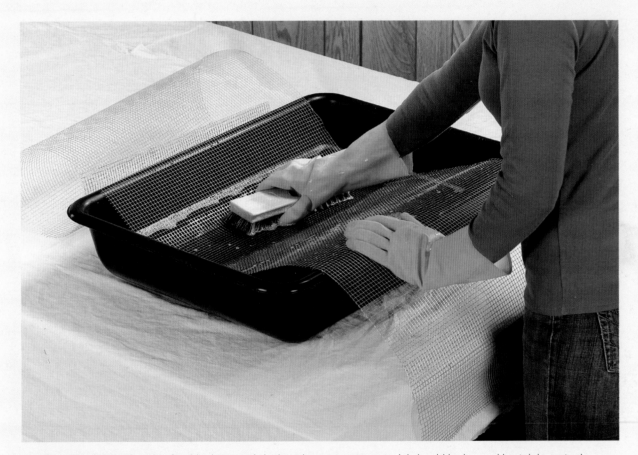

Scrub galvanized wire mesh with vinegar. Birds that chew on cage material should be housed in stainless steel.

and upright with glue and one 3" deck screw. Check each corner for square with a carpenter's square. Also measure diagonally across the frame both ways. If the measurements are not identical, adjust the frame until they are.

Repeat the above steps to make the back frame.

Complete the structural frame assembly by gluing and fastening the front and back frames to the side frame members. Use two screws at each corner to attach the bases and one screw at each corner to attach the top frames. Glue and fasten the crossbars between the tops, aligned with the legs and upright. Use two 3" deck screws for each end of each crossbar (photo C). Stand the structure upright. Measure across all the diagonals and adjust for squareness. Allow the glue to dry overnight.

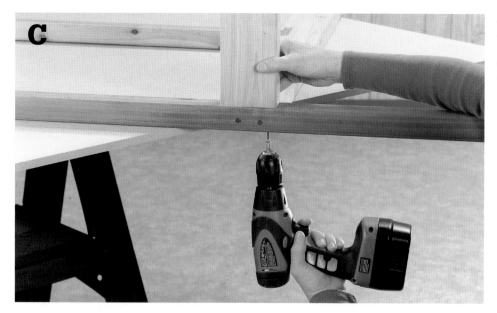

C

Attach the front and back assemblies to the side frame members with glue and screws driven though countersunk pilot holes.

D

Staple the hardware cloth to the bottom of the base and side pieces. Fold the flaps up before you staple. These will be covered later and secured by the base trim.

ATTACH BOTTOM MESH & FRAME DRAWER OPENING

Clean the hardware cloth with vinegar and mild soap (see page 65). Cut a piece of the hardware cloth 27" × 51". Cut a 3" × 3" square from each corner. Turn the structural frame upside down so it is resting on its top. Place the hardware cloth over the base and side pieces. Staple the hardware cloth to the bottom of the bases and sides, using 9/16" staples. Fold the 1 1/2" overhang over the sides of the bases and sides and staple in place (photo D). Use a tack hammer to set any staples that didn't fully set. Screw the remaining two crossbars to the sides, sandwiching the hardware cloth between the crossbar and the side frame.

Rip extra polar stock to 1/2 × 1/2" or purchase two 24" pieces of square 1/2 × 1/2" hardwood molding to make the drawer guides. Cut the guides to length and cut the drawer bottom panel to size from 1/2" plywood. Lay the aviary frame down on its side. Align the drawer guides with the top and bottom of the crossbar. The space between the drawer guides needs to be the actual thickness of the plywood drawer bottom, plus 1/16". Sand or rip the top drawer guide to achieve this spacing. Drill 1/16"-dia. pilot holes in the drawer guides. Glue the drawer guides in place and secure with 1 1/2" finish nails (photo E). Set the nail heads flush with the surface. Repeat with the opposite side drawer guides.

Place the structural frame on its back. Slide the drawer between the drawer guides to confirm that the spacing is correct. Remove the drawer. Allow the glue to dry and then seal the frame and drawer top with polyurethane.

ASSEMBLE THE FACE FRAMES

The poplar face frame panels give the aviary a more finished appearance by covering the raw hardware cloth edges, and they also create four access doors. A power miter saw makes cutting precise miters easier.

Cut the 1 × 2 face frame pieces to length, mitering the ends at 45°. Cut the wider (2½") face frame pieces to length. Because these pieces are 1" wider, they will make unconventional miter corners that feature an offset. Mark the pieces 1" from one side, and cut the miter into the 1½" side (photo F).

Assemble the three large side frames from four L-shaped assemblies of rails and stiles. Apply glue and clamp the part together with band clamps, corner clamps, or picture frame clamps (photo G). Check for square using a carpenter's square.

Assemble the two small side frames, the four large back frames, and the two large front frames. Next, assemble the four small front frames. After the glue dries, secure the frame corners by driving 1½" finish nails in opposite directions through the miter (locknailing) or by driving 2" and 3" screws through the miters. Drill countersunk pilot holes so the screw heads are slightly below the surface. Sand all face-frame surfaces and apply your chosen finish (the parts may also be left unfinished if you prefer).

Drill pilot holes in the drawer guides, then attach them to the frame with glue and 1½" finish nails.

Cut the face-frame members with a power miter saw. Make small dimensional adjustments if needed so frames produce flush overlaps at corners.

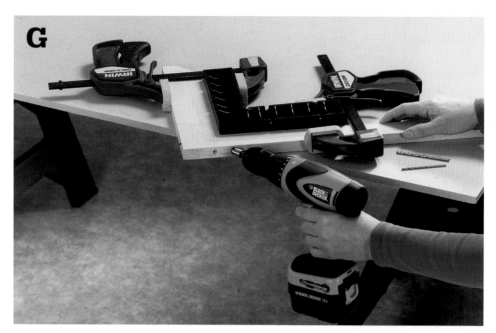

G

Make tight miter joints in the face frames by clamping each corner with a corner clamp. Drill a small pilot hole the full length of the screw; then drill a slightly larger clearance hole in the top piece only, followed by a countersink for the screw head.

H

Position the fixed and operating frames so that a slight gap exists between the operating frame and surrounding fixed frames.

ATTACH MESH & FACE FRAMES

Clean the hardware cloth with vinegar and soapy water (see page 65). Cut pieces of the cloth to fit over the top, back, and one side. Staple in place with ⁹⁄₁₆" staples.

Lay the structural frame on its back. Lay out the fixed and operable frames on the front. Mark the outlines of the operable frames. Cut the hardware cloth so that there are cutouts for each of the three operable frames. Staple the cloth to the structural frame.

Cut hardware cloth to fit the operable frames and staple to the frames.

Repeat the above two steps for the operable frame on the side. Beginning at the top, attach the fixed frames to the structural frame, using finish nails. Place the moveable frames and attach to the fixed frame above each with hinges. Allow a slight gap between the moveable frame and the fixed frames; check as you go that the moveable frame can open and close freely. Continue until all the frames are in place (photo H).

ATTACH BASE TRIM & DRAWER FACE

Cut the base trim pieces. These pieces are mitered across the board thickness, so it is best to miter one end, align the trim piece, and mark the second end for mitering.

Starting at the side with the operable frame, nail the base trim to the aviary, leaving a slight gap beneath the face frames so the doors can pass without friction when they are opened (photo I).

The front base trim is cut into three sections: a pair of short returns on the ends to cover the leg area and the ends of the side trim and a long midsection that has a dual function as a drawer front for the slide-out bottom panel. Slide the drawer between the drawer glides. Apply a bead of glue to the front edge of the drawer. Place the front trim against the drawer, aligning it carefully with the side trim. Drill countersunk pilot holes and attach the drawer front to the drawer with four 2" screws. Plug screw holes with dowels and sand smooth.

Install drawer pulls. Install latches on all operable frames. Cover the top of the clean-out drawer with contact paper.

FINISHING TOUCHES

Place full-spectrum fluorescent lights directly above the cage. You can create a matching wooden enclosure for the fixtures. Attach natural-branch perches that encourage flight across aviary and allow for basking under full light (photo J). Attach the feeder and water supply.

Add the base trim. For a tight fit, it's best to measure and cut the base trim as you go. Because of the miters, the length of this board exceeds the length of the framing by two times its thickness.

Perches should be made of natural branches that have been sterilized. For more information on perches, see the following project.

Bird Perch

When it comes to perches, variety is key. Rope, cuttlebone, wood—flat, round, irregular—it's about mixing it up, preventing repetitive stress injury, and warding off the daily grind of the same smooth ⅜" dowel. That is the beauty of natural branch perches. Every perch, every spot on a perch, is a little different. The safest way to make a natural perch is to purchase sterilized manzanita branches from a pet store or on the Internet. But again, let's not be boring. Below we'll show you how to make natural perches from wood you can find in your own backyard.

Tools
Framing square
Measuring stick
Handsaw
Drill
Box or socket wrench

Materials
Suitable branches (see sidebar)
Hanger bolts (diameter suitable to perch diameter)
Stainless steel fender washers
Locking nuts (nylon inserts) to fit hanger bolts
Cap nut to fit hanger bolt
Bleach

How to select branches for perches ▶

Captive birds are very sensitive to toxins and irritants. Use branches from trees that have not been sprayed with pesticides. Many trees produce toxins naturally. Select branches from our list of safe trees, below.

Branch diameter should be selected so that the bird's claws partially encircle the perch. Perches that are too narrow can result in foot injuries caused by the bird's own claws. Providing a mix of perch diameters, materials, and shapes can help prevent repetitive stress injuries.

Typical perch diameter ranges:
Small birds (finches, canaries and parakeets): 1/2" to 1".
Medium birds (cockatiels, lovebirds and conures): 3/4" to 1 1/2".
Large birds (Amazons): 1 1/2" to 2 1/2".
Very large birds (Macaws): 2" to 3".

Some good woods for perches
Acacia , Sugar Maple, Birch, Elm, Manzanita, Sweet Gum, Eucalyptus, Mock Orange, Staghorn Sumac, Ash, Fir, Mulberry, Sycamore, Aspen, Ginkgo, Pear, Sweet Gum, Bamboo, Grape Vine, Pine (not Pitch Pine), Sycamore, Camellia, Hawthorn, Poplar, Viburnum, Cottonwood, Larch, Rubber Plant, Weeping Willow, Crabapple, Lilac, Russian Olive, Wiegela, Dogwood , Madrone, Silk Tree, Yucca, Dracaena, Magnolia, Spruce, Ailanthus.

Unsuitable woods for perches
Andromeda, Elderberry, Horse Chestnut, Peach, Witch Hazel, Apricot, Euonymus, Juniper, Wisteria, Avacado, Euphorbia, Kentucky Coffee Tree, Plum, Yew, Azalea, Flame Tree, Kumquat, Privet, Black Locust, Weeping Fig, Laurel, Rain Tree, Boxwood, Firethorn (Pyracantha), Lemon, Red Maple, Buckthorn, Golden Chain Tree (Laburnum), Lime, Cedar, Hemlock, Mountain Laurel, Rhododendron, Cherry, Holly, Myrtle, Umbrella Tree, Box Elder, Honey Locust, Nectarine, Walnut.

How to Make a Branch Perch

Determine the attachment points of a perch first. These dictate the length and cut angles of your perch.

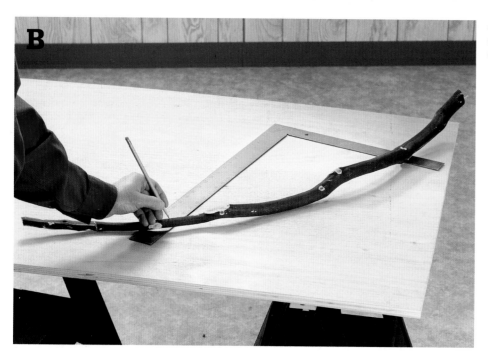

A framing square helps you determine the position and angle of your cuts for a corner perch.

DETERMINE PERCH PLACEMENT AND SIZE

Plan your aviary perches to maximize flight length between perches. Do not place perches above food and water sources. Place at least one perch about 6" below a full spectrum light, if you have one.

If your perch will be perpendicular to the cage sides, measure the distance between cage sides.

For corner perches secured between adjacent walls, measure the distances from the cage corner to the spot where the perch will attach at each end (photo A).

Place a cap-nut over the machine threaded end of the hanger bolt and drive the wood threads into the perch.

CUT AND CLEAN PERCH

Obtain branches of an appropriate species and thickness (see sidebar, page 71). Cut perpendicular perches square to length, resulting in opposite ends that are in a parallel plane. For corner perches, hold the branch to a framing square at the desired distances from the corner. Align the cuts with the arms of the framing square and mark cutting lines (photo B).

Scrub perch branches in soapy water and rinse thoroughly. Bark from "safe" tree species may be left on. Soak the perches in a 10% bleach solution for an hour or more, then bake in a 350° oven for 30 minutes to kill bacteria and micro-organisms.

MOUNT THE PERCH

Drill holes in the ends of the perch. Use a bit about the thickness of the hanger-bolt shaft (below the wood threads).

Put a cap nut on the end of each hanger bolt. Grip the nut with a wrench and drive the wood threads into the perch until buried (photo C).

Put two fender washers and a locking nut on each bolt and cut off the excess bolt. Leave enough excess length for the thickness of the cage.

Remove the nut and one of the washers to position the perch in the cage fabric. Replace the outside washer and nut after threading the bolts through cage bars or grids and tighten (photo D).

Tightening the nut compresses the cage wire between fender washers and prevents movement of the perch.

Ranch Doghouse

Close your eyes and picture the first image that comes to mind when you think of a doghouse. More than likely it's a boxy, boring little structure. Now consider this updated doghouse, with its sheltered breezeway and contemporary styling. What dog wouldn't want to call this distinctive dwelling home? The sturdy 2 × 4 frame provides a stable foundation for the wall panels and roof. The main area has plenty of room to house an average-sized dog comfortably, and the porch area shelters the entry, while providing an open, shady area for your pet to relax. The rounded feet keep the inside of the house dry by raising the base up off the ground.

OVERALL SIZE:
30" HIGH
27¼" WIDE
48" LONG

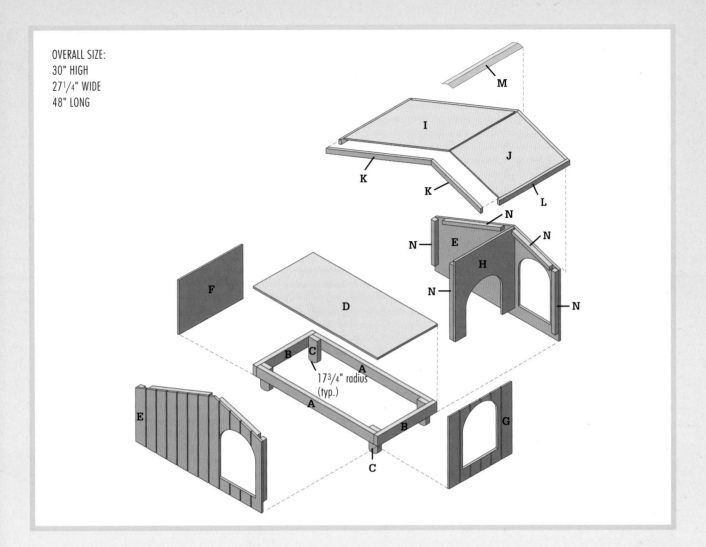

17³/4" radius
(typ.)

Materials

2" and 3" deck screws
6d galvanized finish nails
2d galvanized common nails
Silicone caulk
Roofing nails with rubber washers
Finishing materials
(2) 1 × 2" × 8' cedar
(3) 2 × 2" × 8' pine
(2) 2 × 4" × 8' cedar
(2) ⁵/8" × 4 × 8' siding
(1) ³/4" × 4 × 8' cedar plywood

Cutting List

Key	Part	Dimension	Pcs.	Material
A	Frame side	1¹/2 × 3¹/2 × 45"	2	Cedar
B	Frame end	1¹/2 × 3¹/2 × 22⁷/8"	2	Cedar
C	Feet	1¹/2 × 3¹/2 × 7¹/2"	4	Cedar
D	Floor	³/4 × 22⁷/8 × 48"	1	Cedar plywood
E	Side panel	⁵/8 × 30 × 48"	2	Siding
F	House end panel	⁵/8 × 18 × 24"	1	Siding
G	Porch end panel	⁵/8 × 24 × 24"	1	Siding
H	Center panel	⁵/8 × 22⁷/8 × 29³/4"	1	Siding
I	House roof	³/4 × 25¹/2 × 35"	1	Cedar plywood
J	Porch roof	³/4 × 25¹/2 × 23"	1	Cedar plywood
K	Side roof trim	⁷/8 × 1¹/2 × *"	4	Cedar
L	End roof trim	⁷/8 × 1¹/2 × 27¹/4"	2	Cedar
M	Flashing	¹/16 × 4 × 27¹/4"	1	Galv. flashing
N	Cleat	1¹/2 × 1¹/2 × *"	10	Pine

* Cut to fit

How to Build a Ranch Doghouse

BUILD THE FRAME & FLOOR

The frame of the doghouse is the foundation for the floor, sides and roof. It is built from 2 × 4 cedar lumber.

Cut the frame sides and frame ends to length. Place the frame sides between the frame ends to form a rectangle; then fasten together with 3" deck screws. Make sure to keep the outside edges flush.

Cut the feet to length. Use a compass to lay out a 1¾"-radius roundover curve on one end of each foot, then cut with a jig saw to form the roundover. Smooth out the jig-saw cuts with a power sander.

Fasten a foot in each corner of the frame with 3" deck screws (photo A). Be sure to keep the top edges of the feet flush with the top edges of the frame.

Fasten the 2 × 4 cedar feet to the inside frame corners with 3" galvanized deck screws.

Lay out the roof angle on the side panels using a straightedge.

Lay out the opening archway on the side panels, using a ruler and pencil.

Cut out the openings in the panels with a jig saw.

Cut the floor to size from ¾"-thick exterior plywood, and fasten it to the top of the frame with 2" deck screws. The edges of the floor should be flush with the outside edges of the frame.

MAKE THE WALLS

The walls for the doghouse are cut from ⅝"-thick siding panels—we chose panels with grooves cut every 4" for a more decorative effect.

Cut the side panels to the full size listed in the Cutting List on page 75.

Create the roof line by cutting peaks on the top of the panels. To make the cuts, first mark points 18" up from the bottom on one end, and 24" up from the bottom on the other end. Measure in along the top edge 30" out from the end with the 24" mark, and mark a point to indicate the peak of the roof. Connect the peak mark to the marks on the ends with straight lines to create the cutting lines (photo B). Lay the side panels on top of one another, fastening them with a screw or two in the waste area. Then, cut both panels at the same time, using a circular saw or jig saw, and straightedge cutting guide.

Tip ▸

With most siding products, whether they are sheet goods or lap siding boards, there is a definite front and back face. In some cases, it is very easy to tell which face is meant to be exposed, but you always should be careful not to confuse the two.

Make the arched cutouts in the front (taller) sections of the side panels, by first measuring and marking a point 2" and 16" in from the 24"-tall end of one panel, then drawing lines from the bottom to the top of the panel, through the points. Measure up 4¼" and 15¾" from the bottom edge and draw horizontal lines to complete the square. Find the center point between the sides of the square cutout outline, and measure down 7" from the top of the cutout at that point. Press down on the end of a ruler so it pivots at that point, and use the ruler and a pencil like a compass to draw a curve with a 7" radius across the top of the cutout (photo C). Drill a starter hole at a corner of the cutout outline, then cut the opening with a jig saw (photo D). Trace the cutout onto the other side panel, and then make that cutout.

Cut the center panel and porch end panel to full size. Use one of the side panel cutouts to trace an arched cutout outline onto the porch end panel so the sides are 4½" from each side edge and the top is 15¾" up from the bottom. Mark an arched cutout outline on the center panel, 3⅞" from each side edge and 15¾" up from the bottom.

Make the cutouts with a jig saw, and then sand all cut edges smooth.

ATTACH THE WALLS & FRAME

Cut the house end panel.

Fasten the side panels to the frame with 2" deck screws, so the bottoms of the panels are flush with the bottoms of the frame, and the ends of the panels are flush with the frame ends.

Fasten the house end panel and the porch end panel to the frame so the bottoms of the panels are flush with the bottom of the frame (the sides of the end panels will overlap the side panels by ⅝" on each side).

Cut the ten cleats long enough to fit in the positions shown in the Diagram on page 75—there should be a little space between the ends of the cleats, so exact cutting is not important. Just make sure the edges are flush with the edges of the panel they are attached to.

Fasten four cleats along the perimeter of each side panel, using 2" deck screws.

Fasten the remaining two cleats at the edges of the back side of the center panel.

Set the center panel between the side panels so the front is aligned with the peak in the roof. Make sure the center panel is perpendicular; then attach it with 2" deck screws driven through the side panels and into the cleats at the edges of the center panel (photo E).

ATTACH THE ROOF & TRIM

The roof and trim are the final structural elements to be fastened to the doghouse.

Cut the house roof and porch roof to size from ¾"-thick exterior plywood.

Fasten the roof panels to the cleats at the tops of the side walls, making sure the edges of the panels butt together to form the roof peak.

Cut the trim pieces to frame the roof from 1 × 2 cedar. The end roof trim pieces are square-cut at the ends, but the ends of the side roof trim pieces need to be miter-cut to form clean joints at the peak and at the ends, where they meet the end trim. To mark the side trim pieces for cutting, first cut the side trim pieces so they are an inch or two longer than the space between the end of the roof panel and the roof peak. Lay each rough trim piece in position, flush with the top of the roof panel. On each trim piece, mark a vertical cutoff line that is aligned with the end of the roof panel. Then, mark a cutoff line at the peak, making sure the line is perpendicular to the peak. Cut the trim pieces with a power miter saw or miter box and backsaw.

Attach the trim pieces to the side panels with 6d galvanized finish nails (photo F).

APPLY FINISHING TOUCHES

Sand all the wood surfaces smooth, paying special attention to any sharp edges, then prime and paint the doghouse. Use a good-quality exterior primer and at least two coats of paint, or you can do as we did and simply apply two or three coats of nontoxic sealant to preserve the natural wood tones. We used linseed oil.

Cut a strip of galvanized steel flashing to cover the roof peak (or you can use aluminum flashing, if you prefer). Use tin snips or aviator snips to cut the flashing, and buff the edges with emery paper to help smooth out any sharp points.

Lay the flashing lengthwise on a wood scrap, so the flashing overhangs by 2". Bend the flashing over the edge of the board to create a nice, crisp peak, then attach the flashing with roofing nails with neoprene (rubber) washers driven at 4" intervals (photo G).

Tip ▶

If plan dimensions do not meet your needs, you can recalculate them to a different scale. The doghouse shown here is designed for an average dog (about 15" tall). If you own a larger dog, add 1" to the size of the entry cutouts and panels for every inch that your dog is taller than 15".

Fasten the center panel by driving screws through the side panels into the cleats. Use a combination square to keep the panel even.

Cut each side roof trim piece to fit between the peak and the end of the roof panel, mitering the ends so they will be perpendicular when installed. Attach all the roof trim pieces with galvanized finish nails.

Install metal flashing over the roof peak, using roofing nails with rubber washers.

Dog Ramp

You can spend over $200 on an aluminum ramp, or get your dog into your high truck or SUV with a ramp made specifically for the height of your vehicle. Carpeting gives your pooch a toehold on the 30° grade. Sturdy oak rails project above the ramp deck for a secure look and feel. If you've got the equipment, dado the deck to the rails for that craftsman touch, otherwise use oak deck supports to provide plenty of strength to the ramp when it is fastened to the rails with screws and glue.

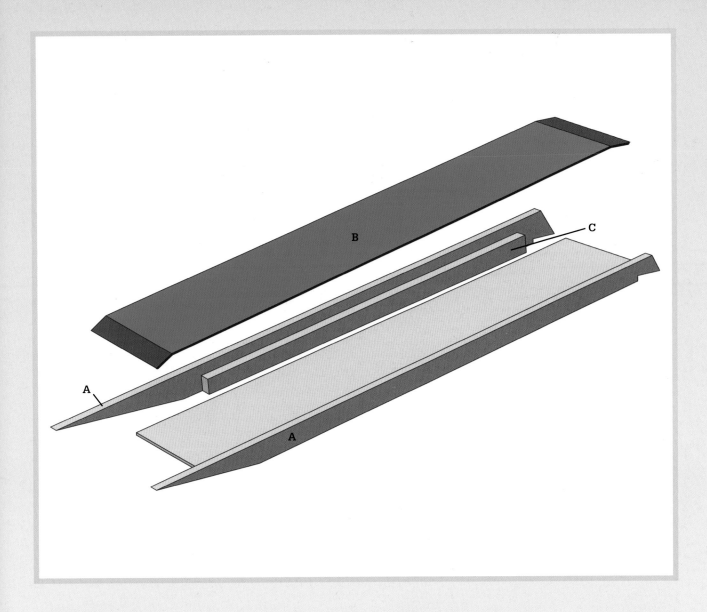

Tools

Measuring tape
Circular saw
Cutting guide
Handsaw
Drill/driver with bits
3/8" countersink bit
Hammer
Utility knife

Materials

Indoor/outdoor carpet runner
Carpet tacks
Carpet adhesive
1¼" and 2" wood screws, exterior wood glue
(2) 1 × 4" × 8' oak
(1) 1 × 2" × 10' oak
(1) ¾ × 14" × 6' exterior plywood

Cutting List (for 30" elevation ramp)

Key	Part	Dimensions	Pcs.	Material
A	Rail	¾ × 3½ × 66"	2	Oak
B	Deck	¾ × 14 × 60"	1	Exterior plywood
C	Support	¾ × 1½ × 56"	2	Oak

Sizing Your Ramp

Vehicle heights differ. The top of the rear bumper on a small station wagon is usually 20 to 24"; small SUVs range from 24" to 28", and medium to large SUVs go upward from 28". We sized this ramp to fit a midsize SUV with a 30" height to the cargo area (the cutlist on page 81 is designed for 30" of elevation). This creates a slope of 27°, which is slightly shallower than 30°, which is the maximum slope you should use. At 66" long, the ramp is about as big as it can be for stowing in the vehicle. If your vehicle cargo area is at a different height than 30", see the chart below to find the overall length of the ramp you should build (if you are a geometry whiz you can calculate the exact size you'll need for a 30° slope).

Required ramp size:

Bumper height (top)	Overall ramp length
Up to 20"	44"
20 to 22"	49"
22 to 24"	53"
24 to 26"	58"
26 to 28"	62"
28 to 30"	66"
30 to 32"	72"
32 to 34"	74"
34 to 36"	81"

How to Make a Dog Ramp

CUT THE PARTS

Cut the rails to length according to the size chart on page 82. Use a strong, durable lumber such as dimensional red oak 1 × 4. Then rip-cut the ramp deck to width using a circular saw, a straightedge guide, or a table saw (photo A). The deck should be 6" shorter than the total rail length. If your bumper is constructed so you can hook the rails of the ramp to it, cut a bird's mouth notch at the end of the each rail to fit onto the bumper. Otherwise, you can leave the ends square cut and plan on using your foot or a weight to secure the ramp at the ground when your dog is on it. Cut out the notches (photo B).

The ramp will be most stable if you cut the other ends (the ones that rest on the ground) so they are parallel to the ground when the ramp is in position. You can use math to calculate this, or simply clamp a rail to your workbench at your vehicle's bumper height and draw a cutting line at the bottom that's parallel to the floor. Trim off this end of each rail.

Cut the ramp deck support strips from 1 × 2 stock (oak) so they are at least 4" shorter than the ramp deck length.

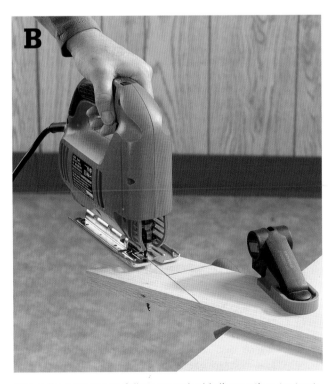

Use a jig saw to carefully cut out the bird's mouth cutouts at the ends of the rail, where they will hook onto your vehicle.

Drill countersunk pilot holes and fasten the supports to the rails with 1¼" screws.

ASSEMBLE THE RAMP

Glue the ramp deck supports flush with the bottom edges of the rails and clamp in place, keeping them clear of any notches you cut for the bumper. Fasten the supports to the rails, using 1¼" screws driven every 6" into countersunk pilot holes (photo C).

Next, glue the ramp deck to the supports and fasten it with 2" screws spaced every 8" and driven into countersunk pilot holes (photo D). The ramp deck should also stop clear of any top notches, and make sure it does not extend past the bottom edges of the rails (trim the deck length if it does).

If you want to get fancy, fill screw countersinks with wood putty and sand smooth when dry. Finish the rails and deck underside as desired (do not apply finish to the top surface of the deck).

You could apply non-skid strips to the ramp to assist with footing, but your animal will feel much more comfortable, (and be more willing to use the ramp) if you cover the deck with carpeting instead (cheap indoor/outdoor carpeting is perfect). Cut the carpeting to fit over the deck and tightly between the rails. Overhang each end of the deck. Remove the carpet and spread carpet adhesive or exterior glue onto the deck. Replace the carpet and press it into the adhesive (photo E). Wrap the overhang carpeting around the ramp deck and secure to the underside with carpet tacks.

Screw and glue the rails to the ramp with 2" screws driven into countersunk pilot holes and spaced at 8" intervals.

Secure the carpet to the deck with an exterior-rated glue or adhesive.

Alternative Joinery ▶

If you have a router or a table saw with a dado blade, you can cut dado grooves for the ramp deck and eliminate the ramp deck supports.

- Cut 3/4" wide, 3/8" deep grooves in the rails at the position of the ramp.
- Glue and screw the rails to the ramp with countersunk screws spaced 8".

Litter Box Conceal

Commercial litter box enclosures call attention to the bodily functions of your cat. Why not build one that's attractive and multi-functional? This conceal features a lift-off lid that doubles as a bench. Make it longer, if you wish, and the enclosure may also hold a bag of cat litter and a waste receptacle. There's no fancy joinery in this project. We show you how to cut and join the pieces with basic tools.

3³/₄" radius

6¹/₄"

3¹/₄"

7¹/₂"

1¹/₂" radius (typ.)

Tools

Measuring tape
Circular saw
Jig saw
Miter box and backsaw

Hammer
Drill/driver and bits
Small roller and roller tray

Materials

6d finish nails
#8 wood screws
Wood glue
Wood filler
Denatured alcohol
Rags
Tack cloth
³/₈" nap roller sleeve
150- and 220-grit
    sandpaper

Primer/sealer
Interior paint
¹/₄" × 2 × 4' lauan
    plywood
³/₄" × 4 × 8' birch veneer
    plywood
1 × 3" × 4' straight
    utility-grade pine
1 × 2" × 10' clear pine

Cutting List

Key	Part	Dimensions	Pcs.	Material
A	Front and back panels	³/₄ × 32 × 19"	2	Birch plywood
B	End panels	³/₄ × 17¹/₂ × 19"	1	Birch plywood
C	Lid	³/₄ × 35 × 19¹/₂"	1	Birch plywood
D	Floor	³/₄ × 32 × 16"	1	Birch plywood
E	Floor front and back supports	³/₄ × 1 × 30¹/₂"	2	Birch plywood
F	Floor side supports	³/₄ × 1 × 16"	2	Birch plywood
G	Lid frames front & back	³/₄ × 1¹/₂ × 35¹/₈"	2	Clear pine
H	Lid frames ends	³/₄ × 1¹/₂ × 17⁵/₈"	2	Clear pine

How to Make a Litter Box Conceal

Draw the bottom cutouts on all four panels with a compass and straightedge (see Diagram, page 87).

Using a compass, mark the 3³/₄"-radius arched doorway in the center of one side panel. The point of the compass should be on a line that's 6¹/₄" above the baseline of the door.

CUT THE PARTS

Cut the front, back, and side panels to size. Cut the lid and floor to size.

On the inside face of the front, back and side panels, draw lines at 1¹/₂" and 2¹/₂" from the bottom edge. On the front and back panels, measure in 2" from each side and mark. Use a compass to mark a

1¹/₂" radius arc from the 2" marks to the 1¹/₂" line. On the side panels, measure 1¹/₄" from each side. Use the compass to draw a 1¹/₂" radius arc from the marks to the line (photo A).

On the back of one side panel, mark the door location. Mark a line 3¹/₄" up from the bottom. Mark

Using a cutting guide makes it easy to cut uniform 1" strips for the floor supports.

Assemble the front, back and end panels with glue and 6d finish nails. Clamp the panels together, drive a nail or two, and then unclamp and finish nailing.

the midpoint of the line. At the midpoint, outline a rectangle that's 7½" wide and 6¼" tall and riding on the 3¼"-line. Use a compass to draw an arc of 3¾" radius on top of the rectangle (photo B).

Drill starter holes inside the lower corners of the door, and cut out the door with a jig saw. Cut the bottom cutouts with a jig saw. Use a straight-edge to guide the long straight cuts. Sand all the cuts.

Use a cutting guide to cut lengths of 1"-wide plywood for floor supports (photo C). Cut the floor supports to length.

Fasten the floor supports to the sides, back and front, using glue and screws.

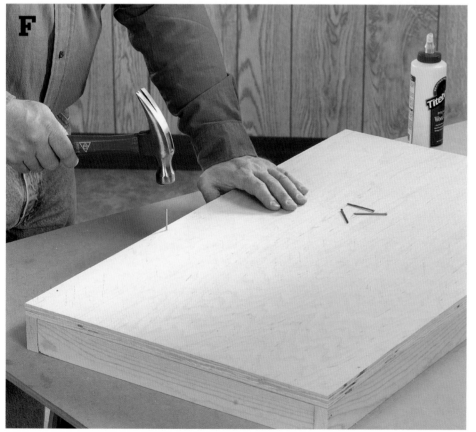

Attach the lid frames to the underside of the lid with glue and finish nails. Set all the nailheads below the surface, using a nail set.

ASSEMBLE THE BENCH

Using glue and finish nails, assemble the front, back and side panels. Place the side panels between the front and back panels (photo D).

Tap the floor into position, aligning the floor bottom with the 2½" line. Secure the floor with finish nails from outside. Glue and screw floor supports to inside sides with 1¼" screws (photo E).

Cut the front and back lid frame pieces. Glue and nail to the lid to the frame.

Measure between the front and back lid frames to check the sizing for the side lid frames. Cut the side lid frames to length, glue, and nail them in place. Set all nails below surface with nail set (photo F).

FINISH THE BENCH

Work wood filler into all seams and nail holes and scrape flush with the panels (photo G). Let it dry. Sand the lid and box using a sanding block or sander with 150-grit sandpaper, then wipe with denatured alcohol on a rag.

Apply a primer with a ⅜" nap roller. When dry, lightly sand with 220-grit and wipe with a tack cloth. Apply two finish coats of paint, sanding lightly in between coats if needed. You may paint the boot-bench/box conceal one color, or a fun variety, as on page 86.

G

Completely fill holes and cracks and scrape off all excess to reduce sanding. A second application of filler after sanding and wiping may be needed.

Cat Sill Perch

Cats love to lie in a window and watch the world go by. But with modern trim carpentry practices, rare is the windowsill that can comfortably accommodate a curious cat. This cozy perch attaches to your existing windowsill without screws, and is easily moved from window to window. You can use any durable upholstery fabric you like to cover the perch. The wood brace can be painted, stained, or left bare.

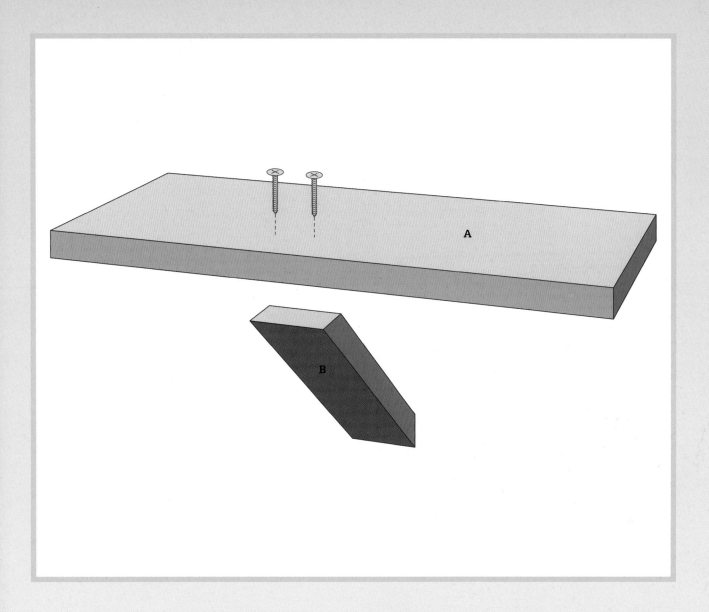

Tools

Circular saw
Measuring tape
Level
Drill/driver
Phillips screwdriver
Carpenters pencil
Scissors
Hammer

Materials

Upholstery fabric
Polyester upholstery batting
3/4" carpet tacks
(2) 1½" L-brackets
Flathead screws
2" drywall screws
Glue
(1) ¾ × 24 × 10" plywood
(1) 2 × 4 scrap

Cutting List

Key	Part	Dimension	Pcs.	Material
A	Platform	¾ × 10 × 24"	1	Plywood
B	Brace	1½ × 3½ × 12"*	1	Pine

* Cut to fit individual window size.

How to Build a Cat Sill Perch

Position, drill, and screw L-brackets to the shelf. Note that the outside face of the brackets projects beyond the edge of the shelf by 3/16".

Cut the brace at a 45° angle to fit against the wall.

PREPARE AND ATTACH L-BRACKETS
Two L-brackets are mounted to the back edge of the platform so the legs that are not screwed to the platform extend down and fit into the gap between the apron and the window sash. If you can find very small L-brackets, or have metal-working tools to cut one down, then you can attach the brackets to the underside of the platform board. Another strategy is to attach slightly longer L-brackets to the top of the platform. The bottom line is that the amount the brackets stick out from the platform must be less than the thickness of the window stool. Attach the L-brackets to the perch platform (photo A).

CUT AND ATTACH THE BRACE
Adjust your circular saw to 45° and miter one end of the brace across the face of the board (photo B).

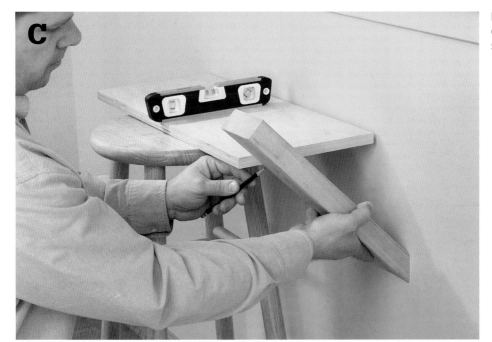

Determine the required length of the brace by holding against the side of the shelf.

Outline where the brace contacts the shelf.

Support the perch so it is level and press the end with the L-brackets up against the wall. Hold the mitered end of the brace against the wall and extend the other end past the side of the shelf. Scribe a line on the edge of the brace flush with the bottom of the perch to create a cutting line on the brace (photo C).

Extend the top of the cut line across the wide face of the brace with a square, and cut it with your circular saw set to 45°. Hold the perch level on the windowsill, and center the cut brace under it. Trace the position of the brace end on the bottom of the perch (photo D).

Drill two ⅛" pilot holes in the shelf on the window side of the brace. Apply glue within the outline then attach the perch to the brace with 2" drywall screws. Test fit the shelf to the window.

UPHOLSTER THE PERCH

Cut the upholstery fabric so it overhangs the shelf by 4" on all sides. Place the rectangle of fabric upside down on a clean surface. Fold the upholstery batting

Layer the polyester batting and the upholstery fabric together.

Trim off the corners of the upholstery fabric to make them easier to tack in.

into a square that overhangs the shelf by 1" on all sides. Center the batting on the fabric (photo E).

Turn the perch upside down and center it on the batting. Cut the corners off the fabric at 45° angles. The cuts should pass about 1½" from the corners (photo F).

Fold the fabric at the corners and attach it to the undersides of the perch with carpet tacks or staples. Hem (fold under) the cut edge of the fabric before attaching it (photo G).

Cut notches out of the fabric around the L brackets and around the brace. Hem and tack every two inches (photo H).

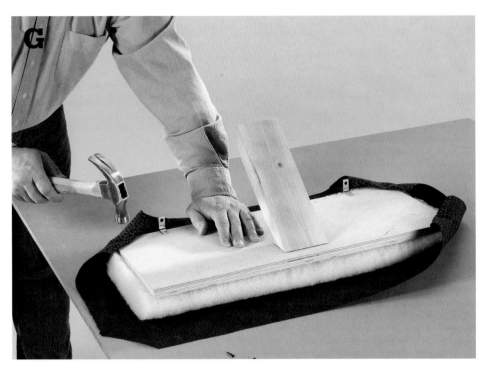

Nail or staple the fabric to the underside of the platform.

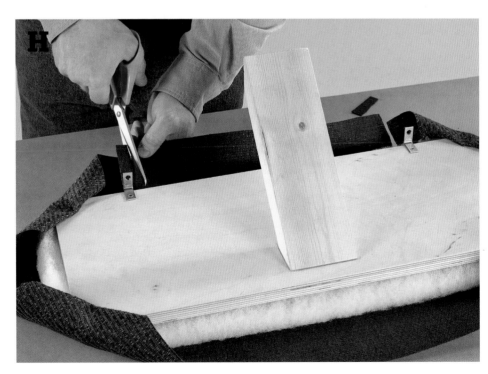

Nail the upholstery in the corners first, drawing any wrinkles out of the fabric on the face of the perch.

Pet Door

Exterior pet doors allow dogs and cats easy access to the out-of-doors while keeping out weather, bugs, and intruders (at least intruders larger than the pet door). Interior pet doors restrict access to certain rooms to the smallest members of the household. For example, they'll let kitty in to the laundry room to use the litter box but keep out Fido and Toddler. For exterior doors, we recommend you spend a little more for a sturdy, aluminum-framed model with a weather-sealing two-part flap.

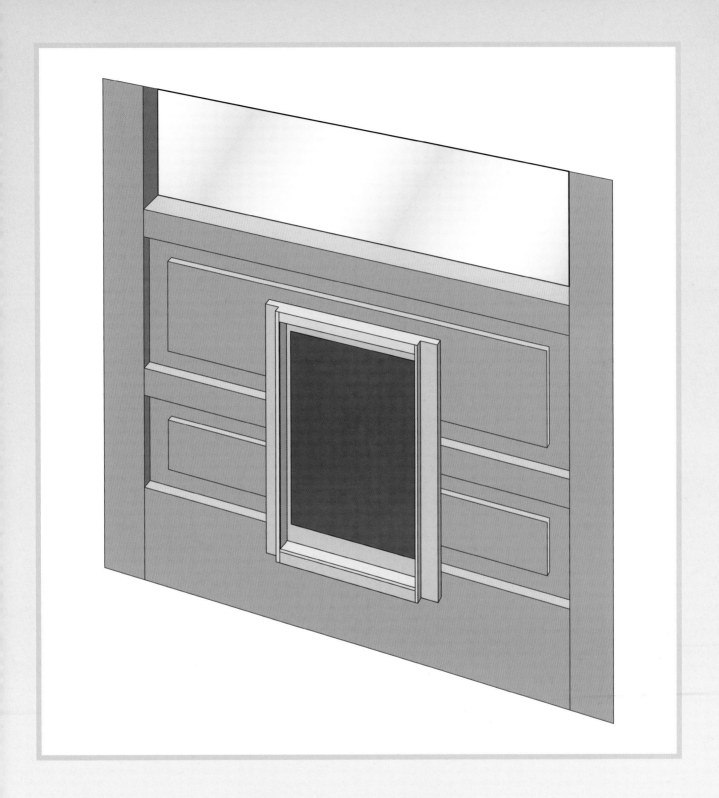

Tools
Measuring tape
Torpedo level
Drill and bits
Jig saw
Screwdriver
Pliers
Hacksaw

Materials
Pet door
Masking tape
Caulk

How to Install a Pet Door

For a dog, the top of the pet door should slightly exceed the dog's full-grown height measured at the shoulders. To keep your human door sturdy, be careful not to cut within 3" of the bottom.

MARK CUTOUT ON DOOR

Measure the largest animal that will be using your door and purchase a pet door that is a little larger. Measure a dog's breadth across the shoulders and depth between shoulder tops and bottom of rib cage (see page 57).

Center the template that comes with the pet door on the lower middle of the human door. The ideal height of a dog door top is about 2" above the standing dog's shoulders. For structural reasons, the cutout should not fall below 3" from the bottom of the human door (photo A).

Check the template for centeredness with a measuring tape. Level with a torpedo level, tape in place, and draw cutout lines and bolt hole locations. Remove the template.

DRILL BOLT HOLES AND CUT OPENING IN DOOR

Drill prescribed boltholes. Next drill starter holes just inside the corners of the cutout rectangle for the jig saw blade.

If the door is metal, pound a dimple into the surface at each hole location with a nail, and then drill through with progressively larger bits until you can fit your saw blade through.

Cut along the side and bottom cutout lines with a jig saw. Cut the top side last. Tape the cutout in the door as you go to support it and to keep it from splintering or tearing (photo B).

PREPARE OPENING IN A PANEL DOOR

If the pet door straddles a rail and a recessed panel or panels, you'll need to even out the opening so the door has a flat installation surface. Measure the depth of the panel relative to the rails with a ruler and a board held across the rails of the door. Rip-cut strips of blocking to this thickness out of ¾"-thick stock.

Measure and cut the blocking to length to fill low panel areas and glue pieces of blocking around the opening. Put blocking on each side of the opening for pet doors with both an interior and an exterior trim kit (photo C).

When set, use the door template to re-drill bolt holes. Caulk any gaps between door and framing.

PREPARE OPENING FOR HOLLOW DOOR

A hollow interior door is just that: hollow. Though many have ribbed cardboard or insulating material inside, these fillers have no structural integrity. Use the following method to provide support for the door after cutting the hole in the door.

Rip-cut blocking from 2 × 6 framing lumber to span the gap between the inner and outer skins of the door. Cut to length, glue and clamp the blocking in place around perimeter of the hole.

Re-drill the bolt holes and proceed with the installation.

ATTACH THE PET DOOR

Insert inside and outside door components and bolt together through bolt holes (photo D). Trim bolts and attach flap according to manufacturer's instructions. The exact installation requirements will vary.

If needed, tape the pet door flap up until your pet becomes accustomed to using the door.

B

A jig saw works well for cutting the door hole. Drill starter holes at the corners. Use a metal-cutting blade for an aluminum storm door.

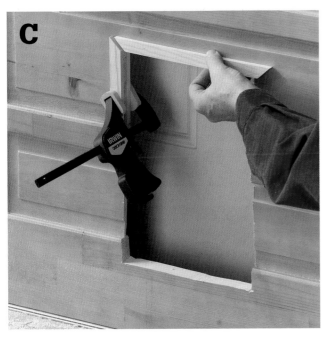

C

Frame the opening with blocking (in frame-and-panel doors); then, fashion and secure frames around the opening to create a flat surface for your pet door.

D

Pet door frames usually come in two pieces that sandwich the cutout panel and bolt together through holes you've drilled in the human door.

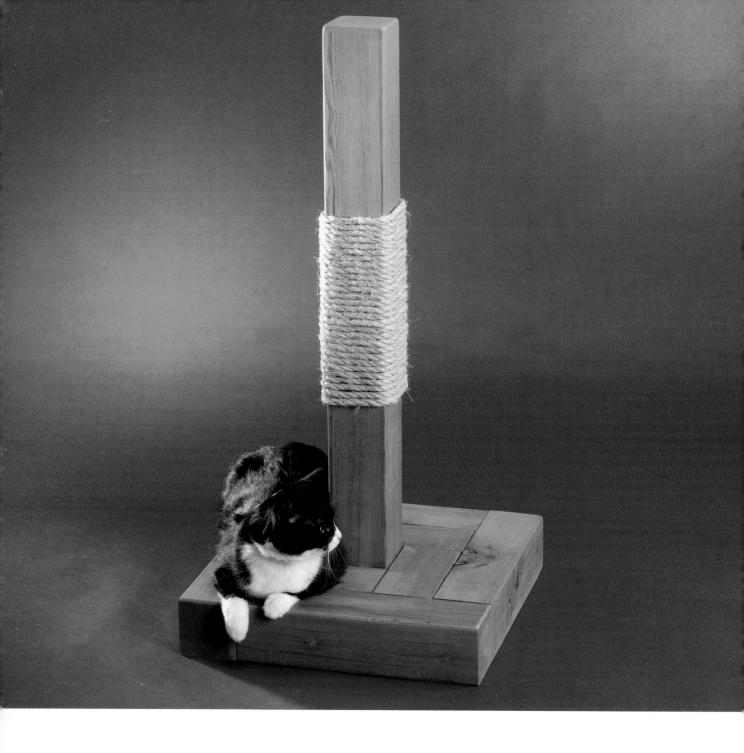

Cedar Scratching Post

Wanted: One superior scratching post, long enough for me to grip up high and stretch against. Must be rock solid, because I don't like things that move (unless they are small and feathered). I'd like it to be made of some deliciously stringy softwood that I can really get my claws into, as I fully intend to destroy it (observe what I've done to your couch). If you can wrap part of it in rope to give me another clawing option, I'd be cool with that. Please put the post next to the couch where I usually scratch, and spray said piece of furniture with nasty citrus stuff, so I'll prefer the post.

Tools

Circular saw
Measuring tape
Square
Drill/driver
Long #2 driver bit
3/8" drill bit

Materials

3" deck screws
Sisal rope (optional)
Glue
50-grit sandpaper
1½" threaded glides (4)
(1) 4 × 4" × 10' cedar
(1) 3/8" hardwood dowel

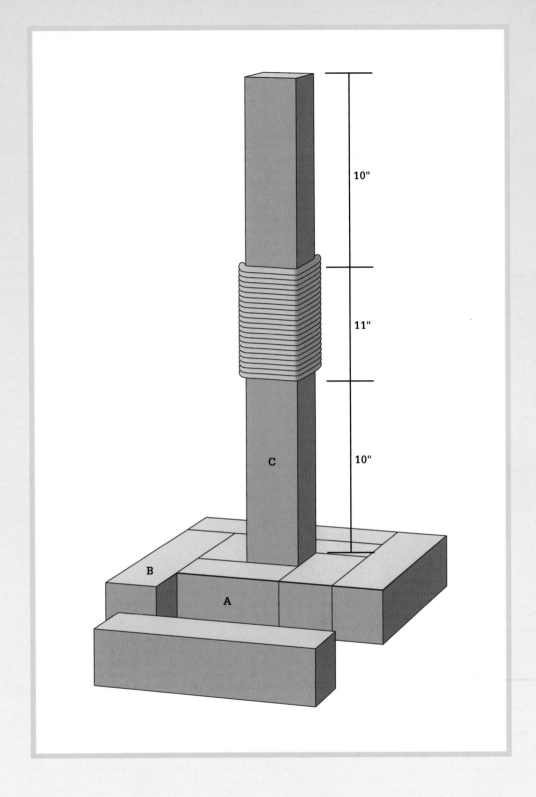

Cutting List

Key	Part	Dimension	Pcs.	Material
A	Inner segment	3½ × 3½ × 7"	4	Cedar
B	Outer segment	3½ × 3½ × 14"	4	Cedar
C	Post	3½ × 3½ × 35"	1	Cedar

* Lengths should be derived from actual thickness of post because of slight deviations from the 3½" × 3½" assumed dimensions.

How to Build a Cedar Scratching Post

ASSEMBLE THE SCRATCH POST

For a good-looking project, it is important to cut the post ends perfectly square. A power miter saw or 10" table saw makes this easy, but a standard circular saw cannot cut through a 4 × 4 post in one pass. To ensure a straight cut with a circular saw, clamp a straightedge or framing square to the post and make the first cut. Turn the post over to the side opposite the cut. Align the saw blade with the first cut and clamp the guide along the saw edge. Make the second cut.

Measure the thickness of the 4 × 4 post. The length of the inner segments is double the post thickness. Cut the inner segments to length.

The length of the outer segments is quadruple the thickness of the post. Cut the outer segments to length. The remaining wood is used to make the post.

Dry fit the inner and outer segments around the post as shown in the diagram. Mark the locations for the screws. Each inner segment has one screw driven into the post. Each outer segment has one screw driven into an inner segment, and one screw driven into the end of the adjoining outer segment.

Drill ³⁄₈" holes (as counterbores) 2" into your base segments in the marked locations (photo A).

Screw and glue the base segments to the post and each other, seating screw heads 2" or more below surface of wood (photo B). Attach the inner segments first.

SAND EDGES AND ATTACH FEET

Chamfer the edges of the base and post top with sandpaper wrapped around a small block of wood (photo C). Glue ³⁄₈" dowel pieces into counterbores. Cut flush and sand (photo D). Drill ¹¹⁄₃₂" (typically) holes in the corners of the base. Insert and adjust the threaded glides.

Do not finish the cedar. If a different look is desired, you may cover the base and post with sisal fabric or rope (photo E), or you can wrap part of the post for a variety of options (see page 19).

A 2" counter bore and a long driver bit make it possible to assemble the timber segments with ordinary 3" deck screws. Attach the inner segments first.

Next, attach the outer segments to the inner segments with 3" deck screws driven into deep counterbores.

C

Chamfer or break the splintery edges with coarse sandpaper and a block of wood.

D

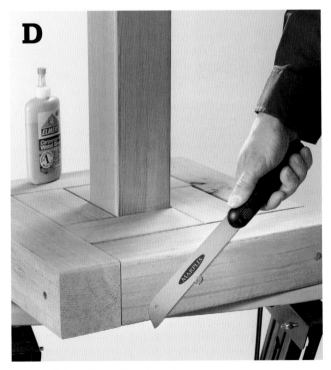

Glue ³/₈" dowel sections into the screw holes. Cut flush and sand.

E

Wrap the post with rope, or a fabric, and nail it in place.

Cat Steps

Think of pet steps as an easy-access cat tree. Even dogs can use them! They may be sized to provide access to a bed or other furniture, or leave them alone for three-story fun for your whole four-legged family. You can even pad and upholster them for the bunk-bed effect, or carpet them for maximum traction. We wrapped the legs of ours in sisal, giving the steps a claw-worthy nautical sensibility.

Cutting a perfectly square end on the pipes is key to the success of this project. If you don't have a power miter saw, follow the directions in the tip box on page 108 to make an oversize miter box.

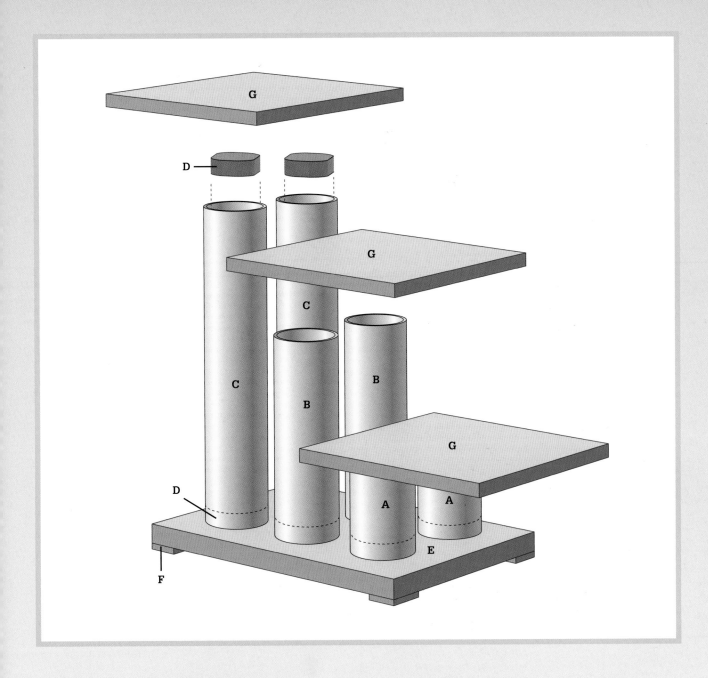

Tools

Measuring tape
Marker
Utility knife
Hand saw
Large miter box
Circular saw
Drill/driver
Jig saw
Caulk gun
Staple gun
Hammer
Panel square

Materials

Polyurethane glue
Construction adhesive
Carpet
9/16" staples
Drywall or deck screws
3/8" sisal rope
Masking tape
(1) 2 × 4" × 4' pine
(1) 5/8" × 2 × 4' sheathing plywood
(1) 4"-o.d. × 10' PVC pipe

Cutting List

Key	Part	Number/size	Pcs.	Material
A	Front posts	4"-dia. × 7½"	2	PVC pipe
B	Middle posts	4"-dia. × 16½"	2	PVC pipe
C	Back posts	4"-dia. × 25½"	2	PVC pipe
D	Post anchors	1½ × 3½" × *	12	Pine
E	Base	5/8 × 18 × 24"	2	Sheathing plywood
F	Feet	5/8 × 2 × 2"	4	Sheathing plywood
G	Steps	5/8 × 16 × 18"	3	Sheathing plywood

* Cut to fit

How to Build Cat Steps

PREPARE BASE AND POSTS

Square cut the front, middle and back posts to length with a handsaw and a large miter box (see sidebar).

In order to attach the posts to the base and steps, wooden inserts need to be glued inside the pipe sections. To make these post anchors, trace the inside diameter of a pipe section onto a 2 × 4. Cut the post anchors with a jig saw (photo A).

Cut the base, feet and steps to size with a circular saw.

Glue and screw the two base layers of sheathing to create the base. Glue the feet flush to the corners of the base and secure with 1" deck screws.

Cut Pipe and Base ▸

If you don't have a power miter saw, make a large miter box out of 2 × 8s. Cut three 12 to 24" lengths of 2 × 8. Fasten two pieces together at a right angle, using glue and 3" deck screws. Place a section of 4" PVC pipe against the L and fasten the second side snugly against the pipe to form a U. Remove the pipe. Mark the midpoint of the box with a framing square. Clamp a straightedge across the open top of the U at the midpoint. Using a backsaw, carefully begin the cut for the miter box. Continue the cut with a handsaw, being careful to keep the cut straight.

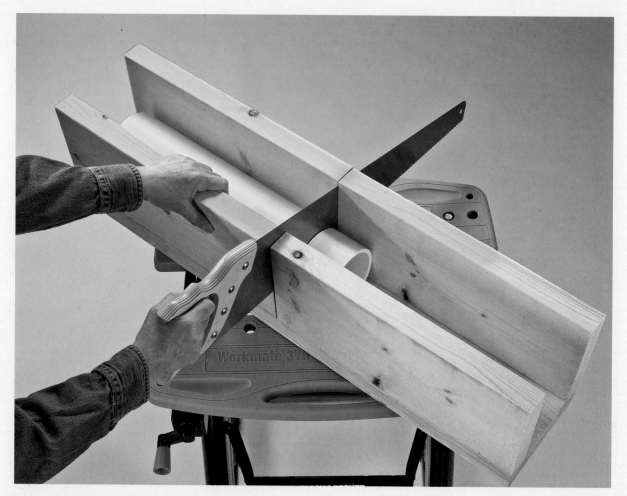

To cut the posts square, make a simple U-shaped miter box out of square-cut 2 × 8s.

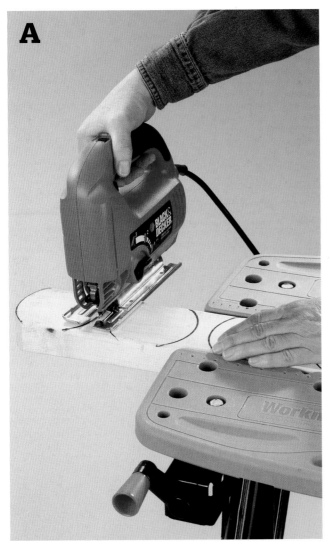

Trace the inside edges of a piece of the leg pipe onto a 2 × 4 and cut out the flat-end discs with a jig saw.

Use a partly driven drywall screw as a temporary handle while you glue and screw the "lozenge" into place.

Dry fit the base anchors in the pipes to check for a snug fit. Adjust if necessary. Apply glue to the round sides of the anchors and insert into pipes, flush with the pipe ends. Use drywall screws driven through pilot holes to clamp the bases until dry (photo B). A screw driven into the base can help serve as a handle, if necessary. When the glue has dried, remove the screws.

CARPET THE BASE
Use a utility knife with a carpet blade to cut carpet rectangles 6" larger than the base and steps. For the steps, cut the corners at a diagonal ¾" from each step

corner. For the base, cut across the carpet corners 2" from the corners (see diagram).

Outline the base on the back side of the base carpet (photo C). Position the six tubes on the carpet 2½" in from the base edge, evenly spaced. Draw the outlines of the tubes onto the carpet back and cut out these holes.

Position the carpet on the base right-side up. Fold under at the edges. Square cut on either side of each foot to allow the big flaps to bypass the foot, and staple to the underside of the base and sides of feet. The outsides of the feet are neatly sheathed in carpet (photo D). Pound any unset staples in with a hammer.

Cut pieces of carpet 6" larger than each step in both directions, then trace the step outline onto the carpet back.

Fold excess carpet under at the corners and staple to the base.

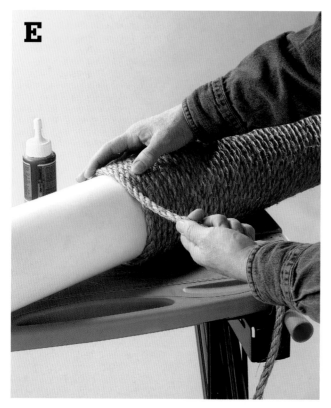

Wrap the posts with ⅜" sisal rope for a decorative touch your cat will love.

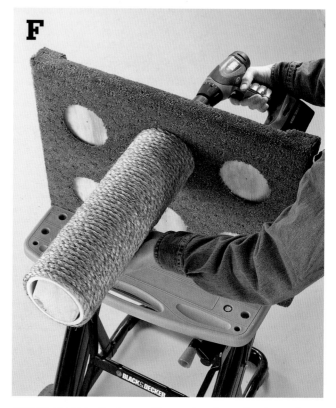

Attach posts to the base with construction adhesive and a few screws driven into the center of the post anchor.

G

Attach the steps to the anchors at the tops of the posts, and then attach carpeting to the steps.

ASSEMBLE THE STEPS

Wrap the posts tightly with sisal rope. Anchor the start and end points with a long thin line of polyurethane glue and generous amounts of masking tape (photo E). Glue and screw all six posts to the base and the steps with construction adhesive and 2" screws (photo F).

Carpet the steps as you did the base, leaving less of an overhang at the corners to accommodate the thinner panels (photo G).

Remove visible masking tape and carve off excess glue when dry.

Oak Dog Bed

A bed frame protects your dog from floor drafts and your couch from the dog. This furniture-quality oak frame can be made to fit any size dog and requires no special woodworking tools. The size of the bed is based on the size of the cushion. Find a rectangular one that fits your needs on the Internet or at a pet store. Then hit your lumberyard or home center for plywood and these nominal-dimension red-oak boards. The bed shown here is sized to accommodate a 30 × 40" dog bed mattress (Note: 30 × 40" pillow-style dog beds are considerably smaller in actual dimensions). This size will be comfortable for dogs up to medium/large in size (75 pounds or so). Always buy your dog mattress first so you can redesign the bed as needed to fit your dog.

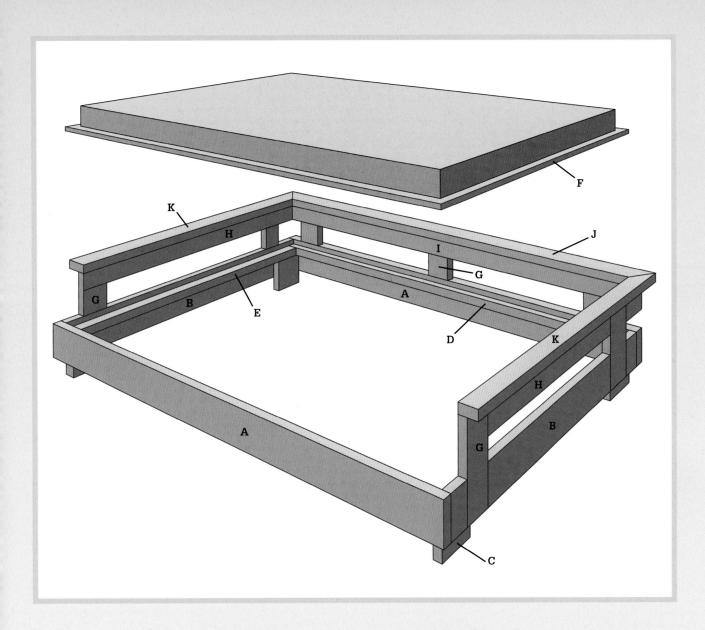

Tools

Measuring tape
Adjustable square
Hammer
Nail punch
Glue brush
Miter box with back saw
Circular saw
Drill/driver and bits

Materials

(3) 1 × 2" × 8' red oak
(4) 1 × 4" × 8' red oak
1/2 × 30 × 40" oak plywood
1 1/2" finish nails
Wood glue
2 1/2" wood screws
3/8" oak dowel or wood plugs
Sandpaper
Finishing materials

Cutting List

Key	Description	Dimension	Pcs.	Material
A	Front and back frame	$3/4 \times 3^{1}/_{2} \times 40"$	2	Oak
B	Side frame	$3/4 \times 3^{1}/_{2} \times 28^{1}/_{2}"$	2	Oak
C	Legs	$3/4 \times 2^{1}/_{2} \times 4"$	4	Oak
D	Front and back ledger	$3/4 \times 1^{1}/_{2} \times 37"$	2	Oak
E	Side ledger	$3/4 \times 1^{1}/_{2} \times 23^{1}/_{2}"$	2	Oak
F	Cushion platform	$3/4 \times 28^{1}/_{4} \times 38^{1}/_{4}"$	1	Oak plywood
G	Baluster	$3/4 \times 2^{1}/_{2} \times 8"$	7	Oak
H	Side rail	$3/4 \times 2^{1}/_{2} \times 25^{1}/_{2}"$	2	Oak
I	Back rail	$3/4 \times 2^{1}/_{2} \times 38^{1}/_{2}"$	1	Oak
J	Back rail cap	$3/4 \times 1^{1}/_{2} \times 41^{1}/_{4}"$	1	Oak
K	Side rail cap	$3/4 \times 1^{1}/_{2} \times 28^{3}/_{4}"$	2	Oak

How to Build an Oak Dog Bed

PREPARE THE PARTS

Measure the cushion or mattress and revise the parts cutting list (page 113) to correspond to the size (existing dimensions are based on a 30" × 40" dog bed). Cut the front, back, balusters, side rail, and back rail to length side frames to length (photo A).

Cut the bed parts to length from dimensional oak lumber (or another wood species of your choice).

The frames and rails are attached to the balusters with half-lap joints so the frame and rail surfaces are flush with the baluster surfaces. Each baluster has a 3½" lap cut into one end for the frame, and a 2½" lap cut into the other end for the rail.

Use a table saw mounted dado blade, a router, or a saw and chisel to make the laps. Directions given here are for using a hand saw and chisel. Mark the width and depth of the lap cuts on the balusters, using an adjustable square. Cut along the notch side of each scored line using a miter box and back saw. The cut is complete when the saw has reached the depth lines on both edges of the board. Cut the edges of the lap cut (called the shoulders) first (photo B). Then, make a series of depth cuts between the shoulder cuts to make it easier to chisel out the waste. All saw cuts should be to ⅜" depth.

Clear out the wood between saw cuts with a mallet and a sharp wood chisel. Position the chisel bevel-side-down at first so you don't cut too deep, then smooth the wood down to the level of the saw marks (photo C). The front frame does not have any lap joints. Make marks for the back frame and rail laps at 2½" in from each end and in the center. Cut the laps. The side frames and rails have laps flush with the front edges and 1¼" in from the back edge. Mark and cut the laps.

Make shoulder cuts for the half-lap joints using a back saw and a cutting guide or miter box. Then, make clearance cuts every ¼" to ½" between the shoulder cuts. All cuts should be to ⅜" depth.

ASSEMBLE THE BED FRAME

Glue and clamp the balusters, frames, and rails for each of the three sides.

Cut the legs to length. Outline the exact positions of the legs and ledgers on the bed frames. Glue, clamp and nail the ledgers and legs to the side frames, and attach the ledgers to the front and back frames. Do not nail into the notches until the balusters are in place (photo D).

Glue and clamp the balusters to the rails and bed frames (photo E).

Drill counterbored pilot holes; then screw and glue the front and back frames to the legs and side frames. Taking care to avoid screws already in the joint, drill counterbored pilot holes and screw the side rails to the back rails (photo F).

Attach the rail caps to the rails, mitering the back corner joints (photo G). Drill a counterbored pilot hole for each screw. The rail caps overhang the rails to the outside by ³⁄₄".

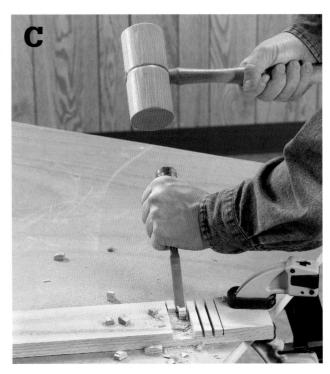

Chisel out the waste wood between the shoulder cuts with a sharp wood chisel. Orient the bevel downward and don't try to remove too much waste at once.

Fastening Fast Facts ▶

The strength and professional look of your dog bed will depend on tight, full glue joints, and properly sized screw holes.

Nail/gluing:
- Paint glue thinly on all mating surfaces of the lap joints and clamp until set.
- Drive nails from legs and ledgers into frames at an angle for strength and so the points stay in the wood. Set the heads of the nails below the surface with a nail punch.
- Scrape and sand off glue squeezed out after the glue is dry. Wiping wet glue can seal the wood and lead to uneven staining.

Screwing Phillips head #10 wood screws:
- Angle top and bottom screws toward the middle of the board for strength.
- Drill a ¹⁄₈" hole the full depth of the screw for the threads; drill a ³⁄₁₆" hole to 1" for the shank, and drill a ³⁄₈" counterbore hole ³⁄₈" deep for the head and dowel.
- Use a #3 driver bit to drive the screw.

Attach the ledgers and legs to the inside faces of the side frames with glue and clamps, and then reinforce the joints with countersunk 1¼" wood screws.

Glue and clamp the balusters to the side and back frames, creating the lap joints.

FINISH THE BED

Glue dowel plugs into the counterbore holes. When the glue is dry, cut the plugs close with a back saw or flush-cutting saw, and then sand smooth. For a bit of extra design appeal, use domed wood plugs on the visible counterbore holes. Break the rail cap edges by sanding lightly and round the rail cap ends slightly at the front of the bed. Paint or finish according to the instructions on your chosen finish product. Drop the plywood platform and dog mattress or pad into the bed frame (photo H).

Drill counterbored pilot holes and then glue and screw the side rail and frames to the back rail and frame.

Attach the rail caps to the rails with glue and counterbored wood screws. Miter the joints where the side rail caps meet the back rail cap.

Glue wood plugs into the counterbores and then sand and finish the bed. Rest the platform on the ledgers and lay the mattress or pad on the platform.

Snake Cage

This box is large enough for a four-foot snake, but you can modify it to fit smaller or larger creatures. Unlike mammals, snakes and lizards are content to hang out in minimally ventilated boxes behind Plexiglas windows. They do, however, need a gradient from warm to cooler within the cage to optimize body temperature. Reptiles also need perch branches or stones to change their elevation, since temperatures naturally fluctuate up and down. Some also need simulated sunlight. Know your particular reptile before you make a cage, so you can plan for whatever lamps and heating elements you might need. Whatever you install, make sure to protect wires and hot lights from your curious creatures.

Tools

Measuring tape
Square
Circular saw
Jig saw
Laminate blade
Drill/driver and bits
Hammer
Nail punch
Caulk gun
Putty knife
Sanding block
Paintbrush

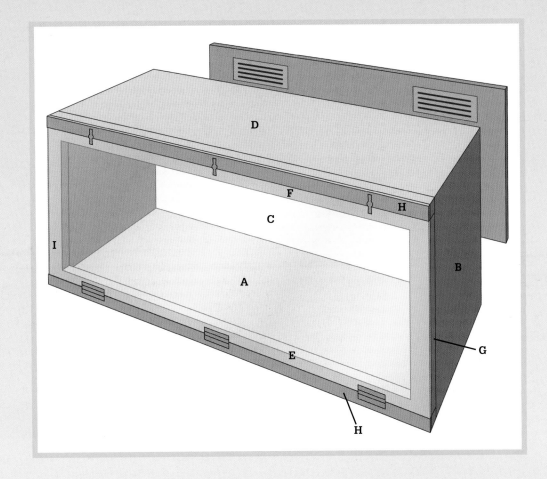

Materials

2½" wallboard screws
Glue
Silicone caulk
2½" finish nails
¾" brads
3 hinges
Machine bolts
Locking (nylon insert) nuts

Washers
Rubber washers
2 metal swiveling screen latches
Wood filler
⅜" nap roller sleeve
150 and 220 grit sandpaper
Shellac-based primer/sealer
Interior paint

3 louvered vent covers (3 × 6")
¾" melamine
¾" MDF
1 × 2 pine
1 × 3 pine
1 × 4 pine
¼ × 2" (actual) oak molding
¼" Plexiglas

Cutting List

Key	Part	Dimension	Pcs.	Material
A	Floor	¾ × 40½ × 23¼"	1	Melamine
B	Sides	¾ × 24 × 23¼"	2	MDF
C	Back	¾ × 40½ × 23¼"	1	MDF
D	Top	¾ × 42 × 24"	1	MDF
E	Bottom door frame	¾ × 3½ × 42⅜"	1	Pine
F	Top door fame	¾ × 2½ × 42⅜"	1	Pine
G	Side door frame	¾ × 1½ × 18³⁄₁₆"	2	Pine
H	Hinge and latch plate	¼ × 2 × 42½"	2	Oak
I	Door	¼ × 42¼ × 19¾"	1	Plexiglas

How to Build a Snake Cage

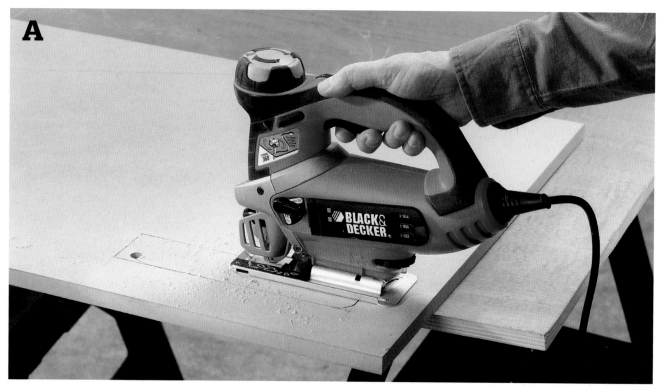

Drill starter holes within each cutout area, then make the vent cutouts with a jig saw.

CUT THE PANELS

Use a circular saw and a cutting guide to cut the floor, sides, back and top to size. Cut melamine upside-down for best cut quality.

Place the vents evenly spaced across one long edge of the back. Trace around the vents. Remove the vents. Measure ¼" to ½" (depending on the style of vent) inside the vent outlines to make the cutting line.

Drill a ½" hole within each vent cutout area. Cut along the cutting line with a jig saw (photo A).

BUILD THE BOX

Place the floor, melamine side up, on a flat surface. Draw a reference line ⅜" in from one of the 24" sides on a side panel. Drill five evenly spaced counterbored pilot holes along the line. Apply glue to the side of the floor panel and attach the side with drywall screws. The side will overhang the floor ¾" on the back. Repeat to install the second side.

Draw a line ⅜" up from the base of the back (the side opposite the vent holes). Drill ten evenly spaced counterbored pilot holes along the line. Apply glue to

the floor edge and the ends of the back. Attach the back against the floor edge and between the sides, using drywall screws (photo B).

Place the top over the back and sides. Draw reference lines ⅜" in from the back edges and drill counterbored pilot holes around the three sides. Remove the top, apply glue to the contact edges, and secure the top.

ATTACH DOOR FRAME

Cut the door frame pieces to length. The door frames overhang the box sides and top by ³⁄₁₆". Align the bottom door frame. Drill ¹⁄₁₆" pilot holes through the frame into the sides and floor. Apply glue to the contact edges, and secure the bottom with 2" finish nails. Attach the sides, then the top door frames in the same manner, remembering to overhang the sides and top by ³⁄₁₆".

Cut the hinge and latch plates to size. Glue the hinge and latch plates flush with the top and bottom edges of the door frame. Secure with ¾" brads.

Set all nail heads with a nail set (photo C).

B

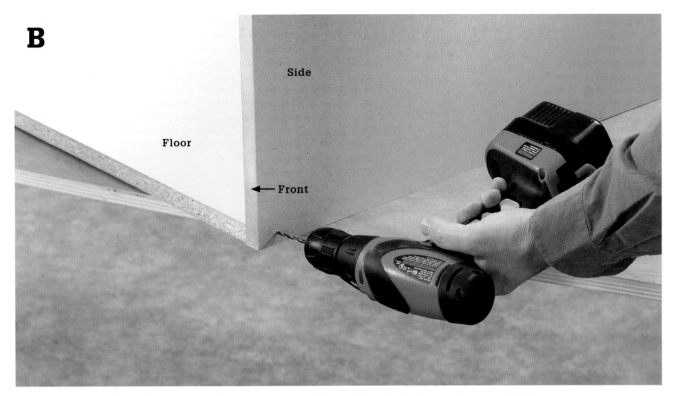

Floor

Side

← Front

Drill counterbored pilot holes, apply glue to the mating edges, and attach the back and sides to the floor with 2¹/₂" wallboard screws.

C

Attach the hinge and latch boards to the door frame. Set all nail heads with a nail set.

D

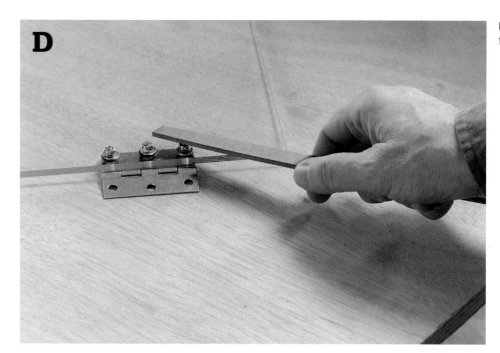

File down the bolts so they are flush with the nuts.

E

Sand the cage smooth before finishing, especially the door frame.

BOLT HINGES TO DOOR

Cut the Plexiglas door to size after building the door frame. You may use a laminate blade in your circular saw, or have the hardware store cut the material for you. Make it ¼" shorter than the distance between the hinge and latch plates.

Space three hinges evenly along the bottom length of the door, and mark hinge-hole locations. Drill slightly oversized holes for the hinge bolts. Use light, even pressure on the drill to avoid chipping the Plexiglas.

Attach the hinges. Use metal over rubber washers under the nut next to the glass. Cut off excess bolt shanks and file smooth to protect reptiles from injury (photo D).

FINISH

Apply silicone caulk to the seam between the melamine floor and the walls. Work wood filler into all seams and nail holes and scrape flush with panels. Let dry.

Sand perfectly smooth using a sanding block or sander with 150-grit sandpaper (photo E), then wipe with denatured alcohol followed by a tack cloth.

Apply a shellac-based primer with a brush and ⅜" nap roller. When dry, sand lightly with 220-grit and wipe with the tack cloth.

Apply two finish coats of paint, sanding lightly in between coats if needed. Choose a glossy or semi-gloss paint for ease of cleanup.

COMPLETE THE CAGE

Place nails under the door as spacers to maintain a consistent gap between Plexiglas and hinge plate. Drill and attach hinges with ¾" screws (photo F). Screw swiveling screen latches to the latch plate

Attach the vent covers over the vent holes.

Attach a heat lamp and/or full-spectrum lamp to the ceiling of the box according to the needs of your reptile.

Cut and attach perch branches and other cage accessories that permit the reptile to bask in a range of distances from the heat source.

Support the Plexiglas door with nails as spacers, and then attach the free hinge leaves to the bottom cage rail.

Aquarium Stand

A good aquarium stand makes the tank and its mechanicals seem to disappear while calling attention to your fish and the magical underwater environment you've created for them. Our example uses a stock cabinet door from a home center and readily available boards, plywood, and molding. We sized the platform under the tank and the valance over it ½" larger than the length and width of our tank. Modify the dimensions below to build a stand for your tank. Just don't skimp on the framing. At about eight pounds per gallon, water is heavy.

Tools

Measuring tape
Adjustable Square
Framing square
Circular saw
Miter box and backsaw
Hammer
Drill/driver and bits

Materials

(3) 2 × 4 × 8' pine
(1) 2 × 2 × 8' pine
(1) 1 × 4 construction grade
(1) 1 × 2 furring strip
½ sheet ¾" oak plywood
½ sheet ¼" oak plywood
18 lineal ft. oak 1 × 2
6 lineal ft. oak 1 × 4
10 lineal ft. oak 1 × 6
5 lineal ft. ½" oak cove molding
(8) 4" metal connector plates
Deck screws
Finish nails and brads
Cabinet door hinges
Door pull
Glue
Finishing materials

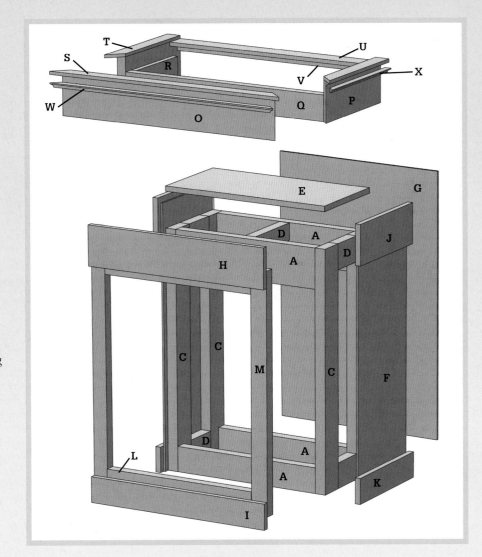

Cutting List

Key	Part	Dimension	Pcs.	Material
A	Frame rail	1½ × 3½ × 21"	4	2 × 4 Pine
B	Door block	1½ × 1½ × 21"	1	2 × 4 Pine
C	Frame stile	1½ × 3½ × 33"	4	2 × 4 Pine
D	Frame side	1½ × 3½ × 5"	5	2 × 4 Pine
E	Tank platform	¾ × 24½ × 13"	1	Plywood
F	Side panel	¼ × 13 × 36½"	2	Oak plywood
G	Back panel	¼ × 24 × 36½"	1	Oak plywood
H	Front trim top	¾ × 5½ × 26"	1	Oak
I	Front trim base	¾ × 3½ × 26"	1	Oak
J	Side trim top	¾ × 5½ × 14"	2	Oak
K	Side trim base	¾ × 3½ × 14½"	2	Oak
L	Door frame rail	¾ × 1½ × 24"	2	Oak
M	Door frame stile	¾ × 1½ × 30"	2	Oak

Key	Part	Dimension	Pcs.	Material
N	Corner trim	1 1/16 × 1 1/16 × 29"	4	Oak corner molding
O	Valance front	¾ × 5½ × 26"	1	Oak
P	Valance side	¾ × 5½ × 14 1/12"	2	Oak
Q	Front blocking	¾ × 3½ × 24½"	1	Pine or poplar
R	Side blocking	¾ × 3½ × 12¾"	2	Pine or poplar
S	Front cap	¾ × 1½ × 27½"	1	Oak
T	Side cap	¾ × 1½ × 16"	2	Oak
U	Back rail	¾ × 1½ × 24½"	1	Oak
V	Back rail support	¾ × 1½ × 24½"	1	Pine or poplar
W	Front cove	½ × ½ × 27½"	1	Oak cove molding
X	Side cove	½ × ½ × 16¾"	2	Oak cove molding
Y	Door	¾ × 22 × 28"	1	Oak plywood

How to Build an Aquarium Stand

Assemble the 2 × 4 frame that supports the plywood platform for the tank.

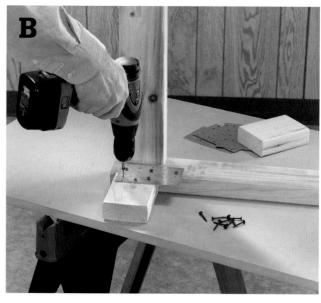

Attach the frame stiles to the frame sides with metal connector plates and wood screws.

BUILD THE STRUCTURAL FRAME

This aquarium stand is constructed with a sturdy 2 × 4 frame to hold the heavy tank weight. The frame is clad with oak plywood and trim. The matching valance on top gives the stand a nice sense of balance, but you may prefer to omit the valance in favor of an ordinary tank lid.

Cut the frame members to length from 2 × 4 stock. Lay out the side members between the rails, one at each end and one in the middle. Drill pilot holes, and fasten with 3" deck screws to create platform frame (photo A). Mark the frame stiles ½" up from the bottoms and align a frame side between two stiles, even with the ½" line. Drill pilot holes

Secure the platform frame to the top of the 2 × 4 frame assembly by driving deck screws toenail style.

and drive 3" screws toenail style through the side and into the stiles. Repeat with the other set of stiles. Align the rails between the stiles at the ½" line, flush with the front edges of the stiles. Drive 3" deck screws through the stiles into the side to secure.

Use screw-on connector plates on the inside of the frame assembly to connect studs to the platform frame and to the base frame sides (photo B). Attach the platform frame to the frame stiles with deck screws driven toenail style (photo C).

Cut the 2 × 2 door blocking to length. Screw the door blocking to the underside of the front rail with 3" screws (photo D).

ATTACH THE DOOR FRAME AND PANELS

Build a frame from 1 × 2 oak to fit around the door opening. You'll get the best results if you cut miters and assemble the frame using normal picture-frame building techniques, and then attach the assembled frame to the structural frame members surrounding the door opening (photo E).

Using a cutting guide and a circular saw (or a table saw), cut the side panels and back panel to size from ¼"-thick oak veneer plywood. Glue and nail the back panel and then the two side panels to the framing. The side panels overlap the back panel and door framing. Position nails where they will be covered with molding.

Cut the tank platform to size from ¾"-thick plywood. Fasten the tank platform to framing with glue and 2" deck screws.

Attach a piece of 2 × 2 blocking to the underside of the frame front to create a mounting surface for installing the door and door trim.

Cut strips of oak 1 × 2 to create a mitered frame and install the frame around the outside of the door opening.

Install oak trim boards around the top and bottom of the tank stand after cladding it with ¼" oak plywood.

Cut strips of oak corner molding (1¹¹/₁₆" molding is used here) to fit between the upper and lower trim pieces and conceal the exposed plywood edges.

Position wood blocking on the inside surfaces of the valance to create bearing points for valance to rest on the tank lid.

CUT AND ATTACH TRIM

The front and side tank trim fits around the platform and the front, back, and side base trims around the base of the stand are mitered where they meet. Check your measurements and cut your miters carefully. Cut the front trim top to size first and attach it with 2½" finish nails or pneumatic finish nails. The tank trim extends ¾" above the platform to create a lip. Cut one mitered end of the side trim, dry-fit and measure for the second miter. Attach the second side trim piece (photo F). Attach the base trim using 2½" finish nails. Cut the corner trim to length from oak corner molding. Attach the corner trim through the sides with 1" brads or pneumatic finish nails (photo G). Set any exposed nail heads with a nail set.

CONSTRUCT VALANCE

The valance rests on top of the tank by means of 1 × 4 blocking on the sides and in front. The blocking is reduced to 1 × 2 in the back to allow room for a filtration system and other tank equipment. Cut the blocking to fit the top of the tank, with the sides sandwiched between the front and the back. Cut the valance front oak 1 × 6, mitering both ends.

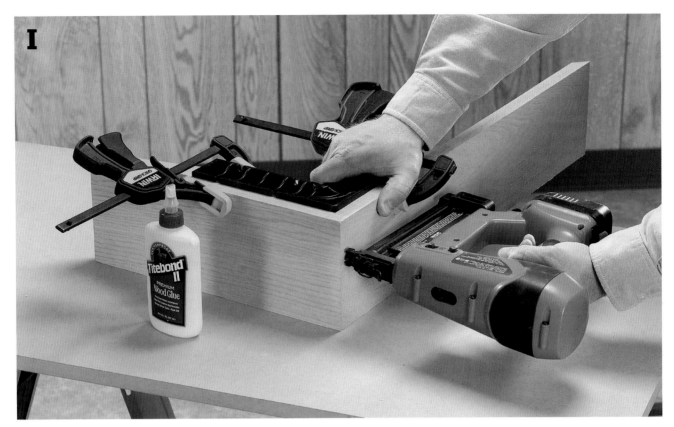

Using a corner clamp to stabilize the assembly, join the valance front and valance sides with glue and nails or screws.

Attach the blocking to the valance front 1/2" up from the bottom of the valance, using glue and 1 1/4" finish nails or pneumatic finish nails (photo H). Construct the remaining valance sides and back in the same manner.

Dry-fit the valance pieces and make any necessary adjustments. Apply glue to the mating edges of the valance and blocking, and then clamp with corner clamps or a frame clamp. Drive nails through the corners to reinforce the joint (photo I). Install the blocking and cap support strips at the back of the valance, just below the side cap rails.

The cap molding sits facedown on top of the valance to create an overhang. Begin with the front cap, cutting it to size, and mitering the ends. Glue and nail the cap to the valance top. Continue cutting, fitting the side caps and back cap. Cut the front cove molding, mitering the ends. Secure the cove molding with brads. Continue cutting, fitting, and nailing the side moldings (photo J).

Make the cabinet door from 3/4" oak plywood, or purchase a door to fit. Hang the door and attach a door pull. Fill all visible nail and screw holes, sand and apply your desired finish to the stand and valance.

Trim out the top of the valance with 1/2" oak cove molding fitted beneath the rail caps.

Cat TV

This vintage-style TV will bring you hours of good clean programming featuring some of your favorite actors. You can build this from a half-sheet of plywood or particleboard and decorate it with contact paper and paint. Add an inexpensive cat pad and other accoutrements to suit your performers and their audience.

Tools

Measuring tape
Protractor
Circular saw
Jig saw
Miter box and backsaw
Hammer
Drill and bits
3" roller and roller pan
Small roller and roller tray
Paintbrush

Materials

6d casing nails
1" brads
Wood glue
Wood filler
³/₈" nap roller sleeve
150- and 220-grit sandpaper
Primer
Interior paint in flat black (front and legs)
    and gloss accent color(s) for molding,
    knobs, and antenna
Decorative perforated sheet metal
Four 12" furniture legs
³/₄" × 4 × 4' (½ sheet) of particleboard
¼" × 2 × 4' (¼) sheet perforated
    hardboard
Wood dowel (³/₈" × 60")
4 ft. screen retainer molding

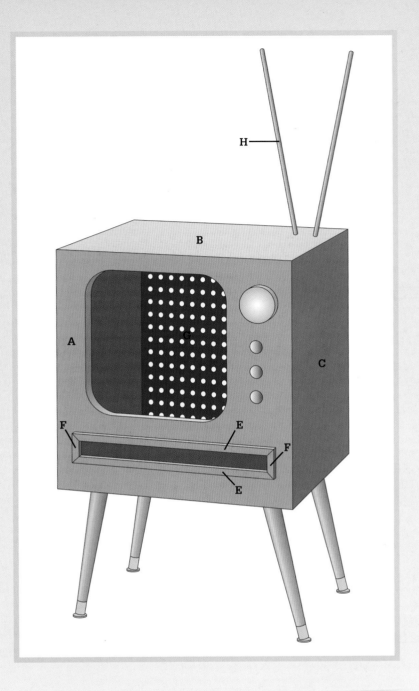

Cutting List

Key	Part	Dimension	Pcs.	Material
A	Front	³/₄ × 20 × 20"	1	Particleboard
B	Bottom/top panel	³/₄ × 20 × 16"	2	Particleboard
C	Side panel	³/₄ × 18¹/₂ × 16"	2	Particleboard
D	Antenna blocking	³/₄ × 4 × 4"	2	Particleboard
E	Bottom/top speaker molding	¼ × ½ × 17"	2	Screen molding
F	Side speaker molding	¼ × ½ × 2¹/₂"	2	Screen molding
G	Back	¼ × 20 × 20"	1	Perforated hardboard
H	Antenna	¼ × 30" dowel	2	Pine dowel

How to Make a Cat Condo TV

CUT THE PIECES

Cut the front, top and bottom and sides to size. Use a cutting guide and circular saw or a table saw (photo A).

On the front panel, draw the TV screen cutout. Draw a 12 × 12" square 2½" from one side and 1½" down from the top. Round the corners with a compass set to a 2" radius.

Set the jig saw base to 15°. Drill a ½" starter hole within the screen area. Then cut the screen with the blade angled inward (photo B).

ASSEMBLE THE CONDO

Glue and nail the top and bottom to the sides with finish nails. The top and bottom overlap the sides.

Glue and nail the front to the sides with finish nails (photo C).

Install blocking inside the cabinet beneath the area you plan to install the dowel antennas. Turn the TV cabinet upside down and glue and nail the antenna blocking pieces to the inside right back corner of the top. Drive all nails below the surface with a nail set (photo D).

A

With a table saw or circular saw and a cutting guide, cut the panels to size from particleboard, including the front, sides, and the perforated hardboard back.

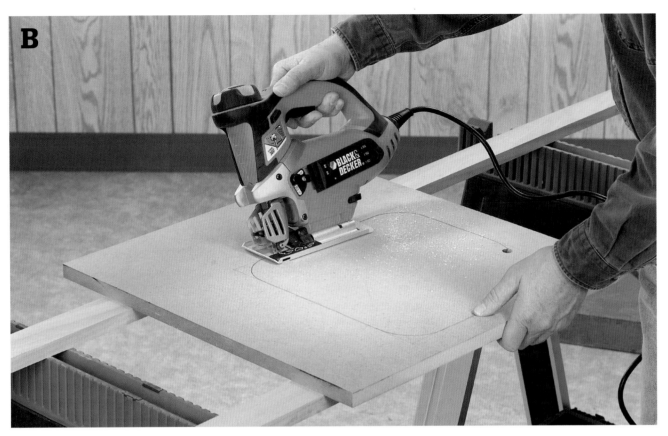

B

Lay out a 12 × 12" square on the front panel and then draw 2"-radius roundovers at the corner to make the TV screen shape. Drill a starter hole and cut out the screen with a jig saw set to cut a 15° bevel.

C

Attach the cabinet sides and top with glue and lid finish nails. The most important function of the nails is to pull the glue joint tight.

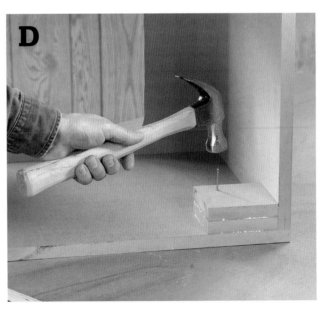

D

Attach the blocking for the TV antenna at the back, right corner of the TV box top, inside the cabinet.

FILL, SAND, PAINT

Soften any sharp edges with sandpaper, then work wood filler into all seams and nail holes and scrape flush with panels (photo E). Let dry.

Sand the outside of TV with a sanding block or sander and 150-grit sandpaper; then wipe the box inside and out with denatured alcohol followed by a tack cloth.

Apply a shellac-based primer inside, on the front of the TV and to the molding, leg, and dowel pieces. Use a brush first for inside corners and accessories then a ⅜" nap roller where possible (photo F).

When dry, sand lightly with 220-grit paper and wipe with a tack cloth.

Apply one finish coat of paint inside and two coats to the face, moldings, legs, and dowels. Sand lightly in between coats if needed.

Stencil knobs or glue on appliqués and any other desired features. Allow to dry thoroughly before papering the TV (photo G).

PAPER AND FINISH

Cut the back (G) to fit from perforated hardboard. Attach the back with glue and nails.

Clean the box surfaces, and then cover the sides and the top of the box with simulated wood grain pattern contact paper. Rub or roll the contact paper as you work, trying to avoid creases and air bubbles (photo H).

Completely fill holes and cracks and scrape off all excess to reduce sanding. A second application of filler after sanding and wiping may be needed.

Paint all box surfaces with primer—even the surfaces that will be covered with contact paper.

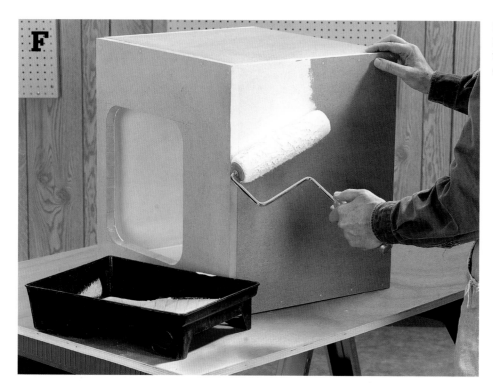

Glue on or paint on the knobs, tuners, and any other decorative features that you'd expect to find on an old console television set. Have fun and be creative with this part of the project.

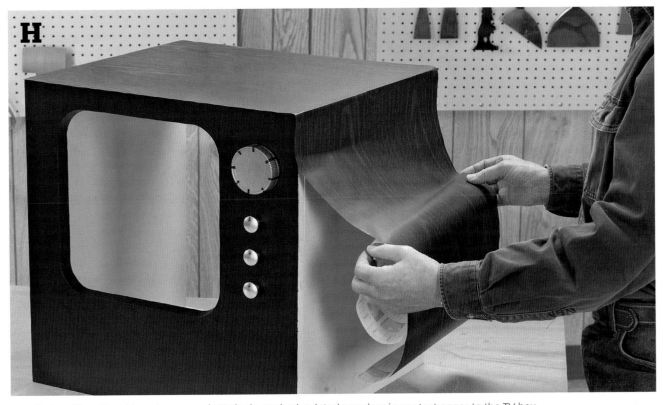

For that authentic mid-century console TV look, apply simulated wood grain contact paper to the TV box.

Focus first on smooth application of the contact paper. Overhang can be trimmed later with a knife.

Create a speaker underneath the screen by attaching a mitered frame around a piece of metal grillwork.

Trim off excess contact paper with a sharp utility knife (photo I).

Cut the speaker molding in a miter box.

To make the speaker, attach a rectangle of decorative sheet metal to the front. Hold in place with a "picture frame" of screen molding. Attach the molding with brads (photo J).

Cut the antenna to length. Drill ⅜" holes at desired angles in the back, right corner of the top at the antenna blocking, and glue in dowel antennas (photo K).

Screw leg brackets to the bottom corners of the TV, and then attach legs to brackets (photo L).

Outfit the inside of your cat condo with a comfy cat bed. If you wish, hang catnip toys around the opening as show props and for your cat's enjoyment.

Tip ▶

For a more finished look, cut rabbets around the back opening and recess the back, reducing its size as required.

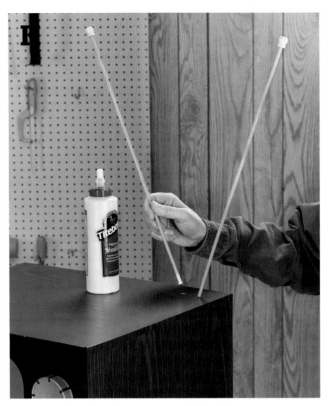

You can simply set a pair or rabbit ear antennae onto the TV, but using unpainted dowels is more appropriate for the tone of the project.

Install prefabricated furniture legs on the underside of the TV cabinet. These can be purchased at most home improvement centers.

Birdhouse

Birds are always looking for nesting areas. Why not help out with this simple house? It's also a great project for children.

Our version is constructed with a swing-out door to make annual fall cleaning easy. There is no perch because it is not necessary.

You can embellish this basic birdhouse many ways, as in the examples above. There are, however, a few important things to keep in mind: don't paint or apply preservatives to the inside of the house, the inside edge of the entrance hole, or within ¼" of the face of the entrance hole or it will keep away the birds. The birdhouse can be hung with simple eyescrews and a chain, mounted on a post, or vertically mounted to a tree or other structure.

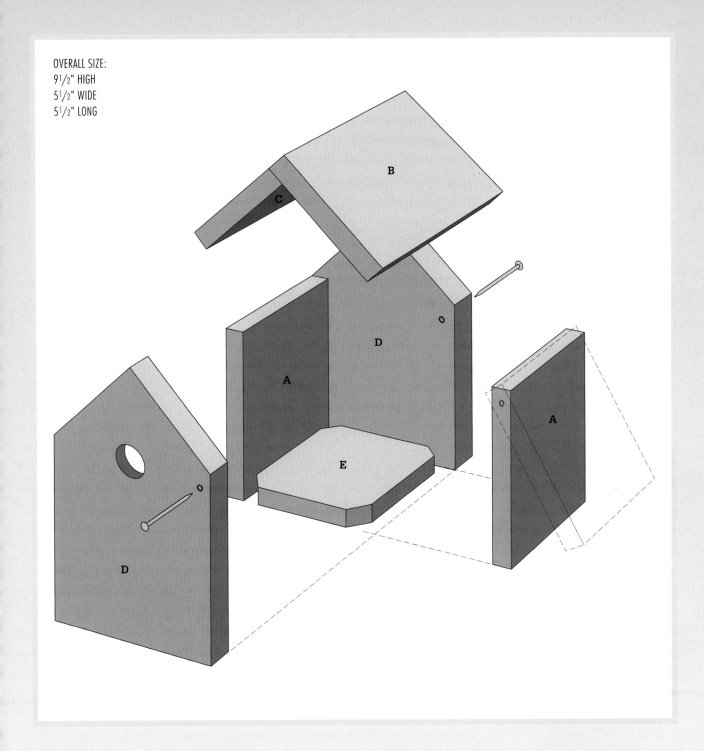

OVERALL SIZE:
9 1/2" HIGH
5 1/2" WIDE
5 1/2" LONG

Materials
4d galvanized finish nails
Exterior wood glue
Shoulder hook
(1) 1 × 6" × 4' cedar

Cutting List

Key	Part	Dimension	Pcs.	Material
A	Side	$3/4 \times 4 \times 5^1/_2$"	2	Cedar
B	Roof	$3/4 \times 5^1/_2 \times 6^1/_2$"	1	Cedar
C	Roof	$3/4 \times 4^3/_4 \times 6^1/_2$"	1	Cedar
D	Front/Back	$3/4 \times 5^1/_2 \times 8^3/_4$"	2	Cedar
E	Bottom	$3/4 \times 4 \times 4$"	1	Cedar

How to Build a Birdhouse

PREPARE THE PARTS

Cut the sides and bottom by first ripping a 15¼" piece of 1 × 6 to a width of 4". Cut the pieces to length. On the bottom piece, make a diagonal cut across each corner, ½" from the end, to allow for drainage.

Cut the front and back to length. To make the peaks, make a mark on each side of these pieces, 2¾" from the top. Mark the center point at the top. Mark lines from the center point to each side, then cut along them (photo A).

A

Lay out cutting lines on the house parts and cut them to size. Draw a reference line on one roof panel where the other roof panel butts against it.

Tip ▸

Different bird species prefer different-sized nesting boxes. Some species, like robins, will not nest in boxes, but prefer platforms on which to build their nests. Many publications give even more specific information on how to attract nesting birds to your yard. Keeping predators and invasive species, like sparrows, from invading nesting boxes is important. Drilling the proper size entrance hole protects your house from becoming a home to sparrows or squirrels. Do not use perches, as these allow predatory birds to sit and wait for adults and nestlings to emerge. The following chart shows nesting box dimensions for common bird species.

Nest Box Dimensions

Species	Box floor	Box height	Hole height	Hole diameter	Box placement
Eastern Bluebird	5 × 5"	8 to 12"	6 to 10"	1½"	4 to 6 ft.
Chickadees	4 × 4"	8 to 10"	6 to 8"	1⅛"	4 to 15 ft.
Titmice	4 × 4"	10 to 12"	6 to 10"	1¼"	5 to 15 ft.
Red-breasted Nuthatch	4 × 4"	8 to 10"	6 to 8"	1¼"	5 to 15 ft.
White-breasted Nuthatch	4 × 4"	8 to 10"	6 to 8"	1⅜"	5 to 15 ft.
Northern Flicker	7 × 7"	16 to 18"	14 to 16"	2½"	6 to 20 ft.
Yellow-bellied Sapsucker	5 × 5"	12 to 15"	9 to 12"	1½"	10 to 20 ft.
House Wrens	4 × 4"	6 to 8"	4 to 6"	1¼"	5 to 10 ft.
Carolina Wren	4 × 4"	6 to 8"	4 to 6"	1½"	5 to 10 ft.
Wood Ducks	10 × 18"	10 to 24"	12 to 16"	4"	10 to 20 ft.

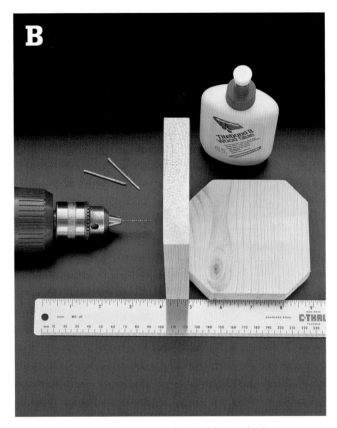

Drill pilot holes and then attach the sides to the bottom panel with 4d galvanized finish nails.

Drill the entry hole for the species you wish to house (see page 140), and then attach the roof with glue and nails.

Mark a point on the front piece 6¾" from the base, centering the mark from side to side. Use an appropriately sized spade bit to drill an entrance hole, usually 1¼ to 1½" (see Tip).

Use a wood screw or awl to make several deep horizontal scratches on the inside of the front piece, starting 1" below the entrance hole. (These grip lines help young birds hold on as they climb up to the entrance hole.)

ASSEMBLE THE BASE AND SIDES
Apply wood glue to one edge of the bottom piece. Butt a side piece against the bottom piece so the bottoms of the two pieces are flush.

Drill ¹/₁₆" pilot holes and attach the pieces, using 4d galvanized finish nails. Repeat this process for the front and back pieces, aligning the edges with the side piece (photo B).

Set the remaining side piece in place, but do not glue it. To attach the side to the front and back pieces, drill ¹/₁₆" pilot holes and drive a 4d nail through the front wall and another through the back wall, each positioned about ⅝" from the top edge. This arrangement allows the piece to pivot.

ADD THE ROOF AND FINISH
Cut the roof pieces to size.

Apply glue to the top edges of one side of the front and back pieces. Set the smaller roof piece on the house so its upper edge is aligned with the peak of the house.

Apply glue to the top edges on the opposite side of the front and back pieces. Place the larger roof piece in position. Drill pilot holes and drive 4d nails through the roof into the front piece and then the back (photo C).

Drill a pilot hole in the edge of the front piece on the pivot wall side, placed about 1" from the bottom edge of the house. Screw in a shoulder hook, positioning it to hold the side piece closed.

Sand the birdhouse smooth, then paint or decorate it as desired.

Bird Feeder

Watching birds feeding in your backyard can be a very relaxing pastime. In this bird feeder project, you will use a piece of 8"-wide cedar lap siding to build a decorative feeder box and then mount it on a piece of scrap plywood. The birds won't mind the leftover building materials. And you'll like the bird feeder, because it costs almost nothing to build. Even the plastic viewing window covers that you place inside the feeder box can be made with clear acrylic scrap left over from another project. To fill this cleverly designed bird feeder with seed, turn the threaded rod that serves as a hook so it is aligned with the slot in the roof. Then, simply lift up the roof and add the bird food.

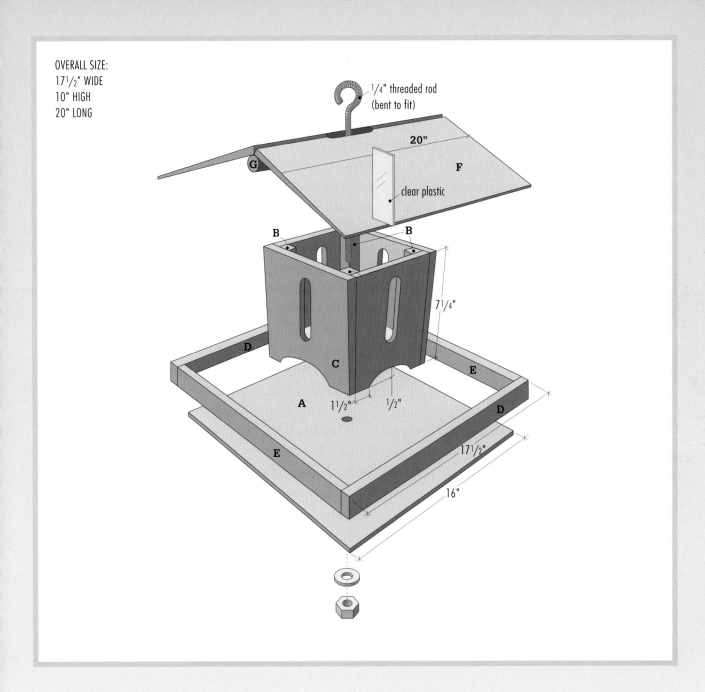

OVERALL SIZE:
17¹/₂" WIDE
10" HIGH
20" LONG

¹/₄" threaded rod
(bent to fit)

20"

F

clear plastic

B

B

G

7¹/₄"

D

C

E

A

1¹/₂"   ¹/₂"

D

E

17¹/₂"

16"

Materials

¹/₄"-dia. threaded rod with matching nut and washer
Hot glue
4d common nails
Rigid acrylic or plastic
(1) ³/₄ × 16 × 16" plywood scrap
(1) ³/₄" × 6' cedar stop molding
(1) 8" × 10' cedar lap siding
(1) 1 × 2" × 8' cedar
(1) 1"-dia. × 3' dowel

Cutting List

Key	Part	Dimension	Pcs.	Material
A	Base	³/₄ × 16 × 16"	1	Plywood
B	Post	³/₄ × ³/₄ × 7¹/₄"	4	Cedar
C	Box side	⁵/₁₆ × 6 × 7¹/₄"	4	Cedar siding
D	Ledge side	³/₄ × 1¹/₂ × 17¹/₂"	2	Cedar
E	Ledge end	³/₄ × 1¹/₂ × 16"	2	Cedar
F	Roof panel	⁵/₁₆ × 7¹/₄ × 20"	2	Cedar siding
G	Ridgepole	1"-dia. × 20"	1	Dowel

How to Build a Bird Feeder

Drill pilot holes in the corners of the feeder box location that is laid out on the plywood base.

CUT AND PREPARE THE BASE

The base provides room for several feeding birds and seed.

Cut the base from ¾" plywood. Draw straight diagonal lines from corner to corner to locate the center of the base.

Measure and mark a 6" square in the middle of the base, making sure the lines are parallel to the edges of the base. This square marks the location for the feeder box.

Drill a ¼"-dia. hole through the center of the base where the lines cross.

Measure in toward the center ⅜" from each corner of the 6" square and mark points. Drill ¹⁄₁₆" pilot holes all the way through at these points (photo A).

PREPARE THE FEEDER BOX PARTS

The posts and box sides form the walls of the feeder box. Vertical grooves in the box sides let you check seed levels. Seed flows through small arcs cut in the bottoms of the box sides.

Cut the posts to length from ¾"-square cedar stop molding. (Or, rip a 3'-long piece of ¾"-thick cedar to ¾" in width to make the posts.)

From 8" cedar lap siding (actual dimension is 7¼") cut two 6"-wide box sides. Then, cut two more panels to about 7" in width to be trimmed later to follow the lap-siding bevels.

Cut viewing slots. First, drill two ½" starter holes for a jig saw blade along the center of each box side—one hole 2" from the top and the other 2" from the bottom. Connect the starter holes by cutting with a jig saw to form the slots.

Cut a ½"-deep arc into the bottom of each box side, using the jig saw. Start the cuts 1½" from each end. Smooth out the arcs with a drum sander on a power drill.

Cut strips of clear acrylic or plastic slightly larger than the viewing slots. Hot glue them over the slots on the inside of the box sides (photo B).

To mark cutting lines for trimming two of the box sides to follow the siding bevel, tape the box sides together into a box shape. The wide ends of the beveled siding should all be flush. Trace the siding profile onto the inside faces of the two box ends (photo C). Disassemble the box. Cut along the profile lines with a jig saw.

Cover the viewing slots by hot gluing clear plastic or acrylic pieces to the inside face of each panel.

Mark the profile of the bevel of the siding onto two of the box sides for trimming.

Tip ▸

Hot glue is often thought of as primarily a product for craftmaking and indoor patch-up jobs. But for lightweight exterior projects, it is a very effective adhesive. The hot glue penetrates deeply into the pores of cedar and creates a strong, durable bond between wood parts.

Drive 4d common nails through pilot holes to fasten the feeder box to the base.

ASSEMBLE THE FEEDER BOX

Hot glue the posts flush with the inside edges on the box sides that were trimmed.

Hot glue the untrimmed box sides to the posts.

ATTACH THE BASE

Align the assembled feeder box with the 6" square outline on the base. Hot glue the box to the base on these lines. Turn the assembly upside down.

Attach the base to the feeder box by driving 4d galvanized common nails through the pre-drilled pilot holes in the base, and into the posts on the feeder box (photo D).

Cut the ledge sides and ledge ends to length. Next, build a frame around the base that prevents seed spills. Using hot glue, attach the ledge pieces so the bottoms are flush with the bottom of the base. Reinforce the joint with 4d common nails.

MAKE THE ROOF

Cut the ridgepole from a 1"-dia. dowel. Cut the roof panels from 8" siding.

To create the roof pitch, lay the panels on your work surface so the wide ends butt together. Place a 1"-thick spacer under each of the narrow ends, 2" in from each end.

Apply a heavy bead of hot glue into the seam between the panels (photo E). Quickly press the ridge pole into the seam. Let the glue harden for at least 15 minutes.

Set the roof right-side-up, and rest each end of the ridgepole on a 2 × 4 block. Drill 3/8" starter holes down through the roof and the ridgepole, 1" to either side of the ridge's midpoint. Connect the starter holes by cutting a slot between them, using a jig saw. Widen the slot until the 1/4"-dia. threaded rod passes through with minimal resistance.

Cut the threaded rod to 16" in length. Use pliers to bend a 1 1/2"-dia. loop in one end of the rod. Place the roof on the feeder box. Then, thread the unbent end of the rod through the roof and the hole in the base (photo F). Spin the rod loop so it is perpendicular to the roof ridge.

Tighten a washer and nut onto the end of the rod, loosely enough so the loop can be spun with moderate effort. For a rustic look, don't apply a finish to your bird feeder.

Insert spacers 2" in from the "eaves" of the roof to set the pitch before applying glue to the seam.

The bird feeder is held together by a looped, threaded rod that runs through the roof and is secured with a washer and nut on the underside of the base.

Bird Feeder Stand

Create a hub of avian activity in your backyard by building this clever bird feeder stand. Bird feeders vary widely in size and style—from small and plain to large and fanciful. One important benefit of this cedar bird feeder stand is that it has a freestanding, open design. Birds are always in full view as they eat. The heavy stand base, made from cedar frames, provides ample support for the post and hanging arms. To simplify cleanup of any spilled food (and to make it accessible to hungry birds), you can attach a layer of window screening over the slats in the top of the base. Cleaning the bird feeder stand is easy—just remove the feeders, tip the stand on its side, and spray it down with a hose.

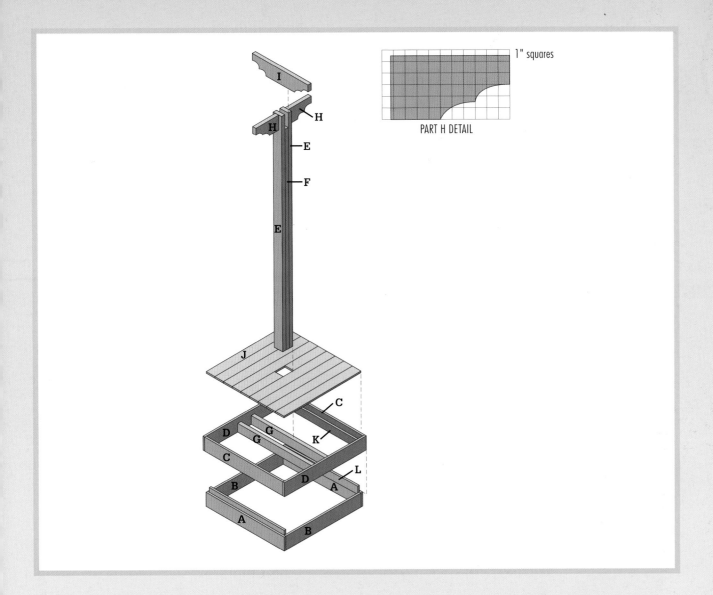

1" squares

PART H DETAIL

Materials

1½" and 2½" deck screws
18 × 36" window screening (2)
Eye hooks
Finishing materials
(1) 1 × 4" × 8' cedar
(1) 1 × 4" × 10' cedar
(2) 1 × 4" × 12' cedar
(2) 1 × 6" × 12' cedar
(2) 2 × 4" × 12' cedar
(1) 2 × 6" × 6' cedar

Cutting List

Key	Part	Dimension	Pcs.	Material
A	Bottom end	$7/8 \times 5^{1}/_{2} \times 33^{1}/_{2}$"	2	Cedar
B	Bottom side	$7/8 \times 5^{1}/_{2} \times 31^{3}/_{4}$"	2	Cedar
C	Top end	$7/8 \times 5^{1}/_{2} \times 33^{1}/_{2}$"	2	Cedar
D	Top side	$7/8 \times 5^{1}/_{2} \times 35^{1}/_{4}$"	2	Cedar
E	Post board	$1^{1}/_{2} \times 3^{1}/_{2} \times 72$"	2	Cedar
F	Center board	$1^{1}/_{2} \times 3^{1}/_{2} \times 66^{1}/_{2}$"	1	Cedar
G	Post support	$1^{1}/_{2} \times 3^{1}/_{2} \times 33^{1}/_{2}$"	2	Cedar
H	Outside arm	$1^{1}/_{2} \times 5^{1}/_{2} \times 10^{1}/_{4}$"	2	Cedar
I	Inside arm	$1^{1}/_{2} \times 5^{1}/_{2} \times 36$"	1	Cedar
J	Floor board	$7/8 \times 3^{1}/_{2} \times 33^{1}/_{2}$"	9	Cedar
K	Floor support	$7/8 \times 3^{1}/_{2} \times 33^{1}/_{2}$"	2	Cedar
L	Bottom cleat	$7/8 \times 3^{1}/_{2} \times 31^{3}/_{4}$"	2	Cedar

How to Build a Bird Feeder Stand

BUILD THE BASE FRAMES

Cut the bottom ends, bottom sides, top ends and top sides to length. Sand the parts smooth. Drill ⅛" pilot holes near the ends of the bottom ends and counterbore the holes to a ¼" depth with a counterbore bit. Fasten the bottom sides between the bottom ends by driving 1½" deck screws through the pilot holes. Repeat this procedure with the top sides and top ends to complete the second base frame.

Cut the floor supports to length. Fasten them to the inside faces of the top ends so the bottoms of the supports are flush with the bottoms of the ends. Cut the bottom cleats to length. Attach them with 1½" deck screws to the inside faces of the bottom ends. Make sure the top edge of each bottom cleat is 1½" above the top edge of each bottom end.

Set the top frame over the bottom frame. Fasten the top and bottom frames together by driving deck screws through the bottom cleats and into the top frame (photo A).

INSTALL POST SUPPORTS

Mark the center points of the top sides on their inside faces. Draw reference lines, 2¼" to each side of the center points. These lines mark the locations for the post supports.

Cut the post supports to length. Place them in the top frame so their bottom edges rest on the tops of the bottom sides. Position the post supports with their inside faces just outside the reference lines. Drill pilot holes through the frame and counterbore the holes. Fasten the post supports to the top frame by driving 2½" deck screws through the frame and into the supports.

Join the top base frame to the bottom base frame by driving screws through the frame cleats.

BUILD THE ARMS

Cut the two outside arms and the inside arm to length. Use a pencil to draw a 1"-square grid pattern on one of the arms. Using the grid patterns as a reference (see diagram, page 149), lay out the decorative scallops at the end of the arm.

Cut along the layout lines with a jig saw. With a 1"-dia. drum sander mounted in an electric drill, smooth the insides of the curves. Use the arm as a template to draw identical scallops on the other arms. Then, cut and sand the other arms to match.

MAKE THE POST

The post is constructed by sandwiching the center board between two post boards. It's easiest to attach the outside arms before you assemble the post.

Cut the post boards to length and draw 5½"-long center lines on one face of each post board, starting at

the top. Then, draw a 5½"-long line, ¾" to each side of the center line, to mark the outlines for the outside arms on the post. On the center line, drill pilot holes for the deck screws, 1½" and 4½" down from the top edge. Counterbore the holes.

Attach the outside arms to the side posts by driving 2½" deck screws through the posts and into the straight ends of the outside arms. Sandwich the center board between the side post boards, with the bottom and side edges flush.

Drive pairs of 2½" deck screws at 8" to 12" intervals, screwing through the face of one post board. Then, flip the assembly over and drive screws through the other post board. Make sure to stagger them so you don't hit screws driven from the other side.

Center the inside arm in the gap at the top of the post (photo B). Then, drive 2½" deck screws through the post boards and into the inside arm.

Install the post assembly by standing the post up between the post supports in the base frame. Be sure the post is centered between the top frame sides and is perpendicular to the post supports. Drive 2½" deck screws through the post supports and into the post to secure the parts.

MAKE THE FEEDING FLOOR

Floorboards are attached to the floor supports within the top base frame.

Cut the floor boards to length. One floorboard should be cut into two 14½"-long pieces to fit between the post and frame.

Arrange the floorboards across the post supports and floor supports, using ¼"-wide scraps to set ¼"-wide gaps between the boards.

To fasten the floorboards to the floor supports and post supports, first drill pilot holes in the floorboards and counterbore the holes. Then, drive 1½" deck screws through the pilot holes and into the floor supports (photo C).

APPLY FINISHING TOUCHES

Apply exterior wood stain to the bird feeder stand. After it dries, staple two 18 × 36" strips of window screening to the floor to keep food from falling through the gaps (photo D).

Insert brass screw eyes or other hardware at the ends of the arms to hang your bird feeders. Set the stand in a semisheltered area in clear view of your favorite window or deck.

Attach the floorboards by driving deck screws through the floorboards and into the post and floor supports.

D

Staple window screening over the tops of the floorboards to keep bird food from falling through the gaps.

Tip ▶

There is a real art to making and stocking bird feeders, identifying species and enjoying bird watching. If you are just a budding ornithologist, make a visit to your local library—the more knowledge you acquire, the more enjoyment you will experience.

Conversion Charts

Converting Measurements

To Convert:	To:	Multiply by:
Inches	Millimeters	25.4
Inches	Centimeters	2.54
Feet	Meters	0.305
Yards	Meters	0.914
Square inches	Square centimeters	6.45
Square feet	Square meters	0.093
Square yards	Square meters	0.836
Cubic inches	Cubic centimeters	16.4
Cubic feet	Cubic meters	0.0283
Cubic yards	Cubic meters	0.765
Ounces	Milliliters	30.0
Pints (U.S.)	Liters	0.473 (Imp. 0.568)
Quarts (U.S.)	Liters	0.946 (Imp. 1.136)
Gallons (U.S.)	Liters	3.785 (Imp. 4.546)
Ounces	Grams	28.4
Pounds	Kilograms	0.454

To Convert:	To:	Multiply by:
Millimeters	Inches	0.039
Centimeters	Inches	0.394
Meters	Feet	3.28
Meters	Yards	1.09
Square centimeters	Square inches	0.155
Square meters	Square feet	10.8
Square meters	Square yards	1.2
Cubic centimeters	Cubic inches	0.061
Cubic meters	Cubic feet	35.3
Cubic meters	Cubic yards	1.31
Milliliters	Ounces	.033
Liters	Pints (U.S.)	2.114 (Imp. 1.76)
Liters	Quarts (U.S.)	1.057 (Imp. 0.88)
Liters	Gallons (U.S.)	0.264 (Imp. 0.22)
Grams	Ounces	0.035
Kilograms	Pounds	2.2

Lumber Dimensions

Nominal - U.S.	Actual - U.S.	METRIC
1 × 2	¾ × 1½"	19 × 38 mm
1 × 3	¾ × 2½"	19 × 64 mm
1 × 4	¾ × 3½"	19 × 89 mm
1 × 5	¾ × 4½"	19 × 114 mm
1 × 6	¾ × 5½"	19 × 140 mm
1 × 7	¾ × 6¼"	19 × 159 mm
1 × 8	¾ × 7¼"	19 × 184 mm
1 × 10	¾ × 9¼"	19 × 235 mm
1 × 12	¾ × 11¼"	19 × 286 mm
1¼ × 4	1 × 3½"	25 × 89 mm
1¼ × 6	1 × 5½"	25 × 140 mm
1¼ × 8	1 × 7¼"	25 × 184 mm
1¼ × 10	1 × 9¼"	25 × 235 mm
1¼ × 12	1 × 11¼"	25 × 286 mm
1½ × 4	1¼ × 3½"	32 × 89 mm
1½ × 6	1¼ × 5½"	32 × 140 mm
1½ × 8	1¼ × 7¼"	32 × 184 mm
1½ × 10	1¼ × 9¼"	32 × 235 mm
1½ × 12	1¼ × 11¼"	32 × 286 mm
2 × 4	1½ × 3½"	38 × 89 mm
2 × 6	1½ × 5½"	38 × 140 mm
2 × 8	1½ × 7¼"	38 × 184 mm
2 × 10	1½ × 9¼"	38 × 235 mm
2 × 12	1½ × 11¼"	38 × 286 mm
3 × 6	2½ × 5½"	64 × 140 mm
4 × 4	3½ × 3½"	89 × 89 mm
4 × 6	3½ × 5½"	89 × 140 mm

Liquid Measurement Equivalents

1 Pint	= 16 Fluid Ounces	= 2 Cups
1 Quart	= 32 Fluid Ounces	= 2 Pints
1 Gallon	= 128 Fluid Ounces	= 4 Quarts

Converting Temperatures

Convert degrees Fahrenheit (F) to degrees Celsius (C) by following this simple formula: Subtract 32 from the Fahrenheit temperature reading. Then, multiply that number by 5/9. For example, 77°F - 32 = 45. 45 × 5/9 = 25°C.

To convert degrees Celsius to degrees Fahrenheit, multiply the Celsius temperature reading by 9/5. Then, add 32. For example, 25°C × 9/5 = 45. 45 + 32 = 77°F.

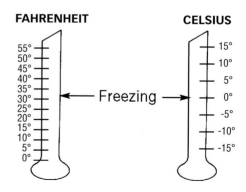

Index